Weight Training
Principles & Practice

Christopher M. Norris
MSc CBA MCSP SRP

A & C Black · London

First published 1993 by
A & C Black (Publishers) Ltd
35 Bedford Row, London WC1R 4JH

Reprinted 1995

ISBN 0 7136 3771 4

A CIP catalogue record for this book
is available from the British Library.

Distributed in the USA by The Talman Company
131 Spring Street, New York, NY 10012.

Acknowledgements
The publishers would like to thank
Espree Fitness Equipment, exclusive
distributors in the UK for Cybex
Strength and Metabolic Systems,
and Puma UK Limited for their
contributions to this book.

Thanks also to The Espree Club
and LA Fitness PLC for the use
of their facilities.

Designed by Rowan Seymour
Diagrams © Malcolm Porter 1993
Typeset in Melior by J&L Composition Ltd, Filey, North Yorkshire
Printed and bound in Great Britain by
The Cromwell Press, Broughton Gifford, Wiltshire

Contents

PART ONE

The Scientific Principles of Weight Training

Chapter 1

Preparation for training

Warm-up

In terms of injury, the preparation you do before starting a work-out can be more important than the contents of the work-out itself. Jumping straight into exercise is both ineffectual and dangerous. Just as a car needs to be warmed up before it will run smoothly, it takes time for the body to 'get going' and change from normal resting levels to a point at which it is ready to face the rigours of intense exercise.

Because the body tissues are stiffer and less pliable when cold, muscles are more easily pulled and joints can be damaged. In addition, the heartbeat is speeded up with a jolt instead of increasing gradually, and can become irregular rather than showing its normal smooth rhythm. These changes affecting the heart can be potentially very serious, especially in an older or less active individual. The function of a warm-up is therefore to prepare the body for action, and in so doing both to reduce the likelihood of injury and to make the subsequent exercise routine more effective.

A warm-up can be either 'passive', during which the body is heated from the outside, or 'active', where exercise is used to form the heat internally. An example of a passive warm-up is to have a sauna or hot shower, while an active warm-up can be achieved through gentle jogging. Both types can be effective, but are appropriate to different situations.

An active warm-up is the type normally used before exercise, while the passive warm-up is useful when working with an injury, for example before stretching a muscle tightened from a previous strain. From the point of view of injury and rehabilitation, the obvious advantage of the passive warm-up is that it does not require the athlete to move the injured tissues in order to create body-heat. Another, often neglected, advantage of the passive warm-up is that it does not significantly use up any of the body's energy supplies. This can be important before competition, when a passive warm-up is used to maintain body-heat after an active warm-up has been performed.

A good warm-up will have a number of effects. First, it will make the actions which follow it smoother through practice. This is the reasoning behind taking a practice swing before hitting a golf ball, for example, and is useful before any activity which requires skill. The second function of a warm-up is to increase the heartbeat and raise the blood pressure steadily and safely, rather than causing them to jump dangerously from resting to training levels. Finally, the warmth produced in the body will increase the flow of blood through the tissues and allow them to stretch more easily.

A 'general' warm-up affects the whole body, and should always be followed by a 'specific' warm-up that concentrates on the part or parts of the body which will be used in a particular exercise.

Warm-up techniques

The amount of activity required in a warm-up will depend on a person's fitness level and on the intensity of the exercise or sport to be undertaken. This is because different people raise their body temperature at different rates, depending on body-size, amount of body-fat and rate of energy metabolism. In addition, different sports will make very different demands on the body's tissues. For this reason the warm-up before a vigorous game of squash, for example, would need to be more extensive than that which might precede a casual round of golf. Equally, a top-level sprinter will require a more thorough warm-up session than a weekend sportsman, because the sprinter is likely to be able to push himself to a higher level of physical activity.

To be effective, a warm-up should be intense enough to cause mild sweating. When this happens, the inside (core) temperature of the body has increased by about 1°C. It is best to perform the warm-up wearing a full track suit or other insulating clothing; this keeps in body-heat and maintains the benefits of the warm-up until the sport is to be performed. Gentle jogging, light aerobics, or cycling on a static bicycle in the gym are all good warm-up activities. The joints should be taken through their full range of motion, starting with small movements which gradually become larger and more dynamic.

Finally, the specific actions of the athlete's particular event should be rehearsed during the warm-up period. For example, go through a few slow shots in squash, or perform a single light set of exercises with weight training apparatus, before going on to more demanding movements. In this way you can practise the complex actions that are to come.

Warm-down

Just as it is vital to begin an exercise session slowly, so it is important to end it in the same way. When you exercise hard your heartbeat is increased, and the process is actually helped by the contraction of the exercising muscles. This system, known as the 'auxiliary muscle pump', is important to the functioning of the cardiovascular system. If you stop exercising suddenly, the muscles no longer contract and pump blood along the vessels which travel through them. The demand placed on the heart is greater and the pulse actually increases, even though you have stopped exercising!

A good example of this is provided by the use of electric treadmills in the gym. When inexperienced users run on these they sometimes get carried away, and get faster and faster until they start to become exhausted. Instead of slowing down, they jump off the treadmill in a panic, momentarily increasing the demand on the heart – sometimes with tragic consequences.

Another important feature of the warm-down period is that it can help to reduce muscle ache. Acids formed while you exercise will cause muscle pain, and swelling within the muscle can give *delayed onset muscle soreness* (DOMS) – you feel fine the day after a work-out, but during the next day you feel stiff. To reduce these effects a warm-down (or cool-down) period should be performed, using similar exercises to those chosen for the warm-up. Start the warm-down at the intensity of your work-out and gradually slow down until your pulse is back to its normal resting level.

Clothing

Clothing for the gym should be comfortable. Loose-fitting clothes are essential for unrestricted movement, but they should not be so loose that they could get trapped in moving gym machinery. Shorts and T-shirts or a leotard are fine, but fleecy garments should be worn during the warm-up and then removed later as you get hot. Shoes for the gym should support the foot and provide adequate grip while allowing free movement. Training shoes are the obvious choice, but specialist shoes designed for one sport do not necessarily transfer to another. For example, running shoes often restrict the sideways movements of the foot and can be uncomfortable when performing some leg exercises with weights. Whatever shoes you choose, make sure that the laces are kept short so that you do not step on them and trip.

Many people wear different types of joint strapping, the most popular being for the wrist and knee. If you have an injury you should not train except under the direction of your physiotherapist. When recovering from an injury and re-strengthening a part of the body, a strapping is not normally used. However, preventive strapping properly applied does have a place if you have a particular weakness which has not responded to treatment. Usually the elastic supports worn in the gym serve two functions. They keep a joint warm, especially if they are made of neoprene; this can be of particular advantage in the case of an arthritic joint. They also offer psychological support by giving the athlete confidence that the joint will not collapse. Provided supports are not used to cover up an injury and work through pain, they are harmless.

Weight training gloves are useful. These are fingerless gloves, usually leather palmed and string backed. They have a padded area over the palm where you grip a weight training bar, and help to prevent the build up of hard skin which occurs there with regular training. Like so many items of sports clothing, they come in a variety of bright, fashionable colours.

A weight training belt is another piece of equipment which is regaining popularity. These were originally used by weight lifters to protect the lower back when lifting very heavy weights. They are thick leather belts, usually about 4 in wide. Worn around the waist, the stiff leather supports the lower spine in two ways: it reminds the user to keep the lower spine flat; and it increases the pressure within the abdomen, which in turn reduces the strain placed on the spinal discs. However, belts will only support the spine if worn tightly, so when you see someone with a bright red belt hanging down loosely over the hips, it is for fashion and not for protection!

Safety

Modern gyms are usually clean, well lit and inviting. Although they look very appealing, however, they contain many potential dangers, and so basic safety standards must always be applied if accidents are to be avoided.

The way you prepare yourself and the care you take with the apparatus are both important. Loose clothing, long hair and dangling jewellery can all catch on the moving parts of weight training machines, taking the user into the apparatus and causing severe injury. Large rings can get caught and slice into your finger. If a sharp ring will not come off, cover it with tape or wear a weight training glove over it.

Exercising in bare feet is not wise. Weights can be dropped and toes can be stubbed. In addition you may step on sharp objects or slip on wooden or rubberised flooring. Thin rubber shoes and flip-flops are little better, and really have no place in the gym even in the height of summer.

Now to the equipment itself. Always check this before use because broken or defective machinery can cause injury. Collars on free weights can work loose and fall off, and stiff machines may be set in motion with a jolt. The weights on solid dumb-bells should always be checked to ensure that they are screwed up tightly before use.

With multi-stack apparatus, make sure the selector key is pushed right into the machine and twisted so that it is locked into place. If pulley cables become snagged, get help; don't try to free them by yourself. Never touch the pulleys and cables when they are in use. Finally, make sure that the machinery is correctly adjusted for your size. It may take a few extra moments to change the settings, but this is time well spent in terms of comfort and safety.

The spine

Unfortunately, the spine is at risk when weights are lifted; however, good lifting technique and general care of the back will reduce the likelihood of injury considerably.

Dangers come from two sources: bending, and fast, uncontrolled movements. In the case of bending, the discs in the base of the spine are squeezed out of shape and pressed closer to the delicate nerves travelling from the spinal cord to the legs. Repeated bending can cause irritation of these nerves, leading to back pain or sciatica. Try therefore to keep forward-bending to a minimum when weight training, and maintain the natural hollow in the base of the spine when standing or sitting.

During general weight training the spinal discs are compressed and water is squeezed from them. This has the effect of actually shortening the spine after a work-out. To help offset this, stretch the spine after training by holding onto the high bar and hanging for between 30 and 60 seconds. It is also useful to include exercises which stretch the spine, such as chin-ups, dips and lateral pull-downs, in the latter part of a work-out that involves compression exercises (for example squats and shoulder presses).

Because bending the spine causes problems, arching the spine can help to offset them. This fact enables us to compensate to a certain degree for some of the problems which may occur while training. The following is one of the physiotherapy techniques known as 'mechanical therapy' (fig. 13, page 43). Lie on the floor as though you were about to do a push-up exercise. Keep your legs and hips down on the floor and push up with the arms, arching your spine as you do so. Look up at the ceiling, pause momentarily in this position, and then lower yourself down onto the floor again. Repeat this movement ten times. You should find that this starts to relieve any back pain caused through repeated bending. Obviously this exercise is not a 'cure-all', so it is best to avoid repeated bending as much as possible – prevention being better than cure!

Rapid movements, particularly twisting, can also tax the spine. Rapid trunk twisting or bending should be avoided because the weight of the spine and trunk builds up momentum. This momentum will tear at the spinal tissues at the very end of the movement, over-stretching them and making them swell. As the swelling forms slowly, you will not actually feel pain until you get up the next morning. Then, your back will be stiff and take time to 'get going'. The best bet in this case is to rest for a few days, and, when you resume training, correct any faulty exercise techniques. If pain still persists, have a word with your doctor.

When lifting free weights from the floor, correct technique is important for protection of the spine. Before you lift, take up a stable position with your feet astride and at least one foot flat. Bend your knees and get down to the level of the weight, keeping your spine hollow as you move. Grip the weight securely, and use the power of your legs, not your back, to lift. As you do this, look up! Bring the weight close into your waist as soon as possible in order to reduce the leverage forces acting on the spine. When you put the weight down, reverse this sequence, always using the strength of your legs and not your back.

Safety check-list for the gym

- Warm up before training.
- Check machinery before use.
- Tie long hair back and take care with loose clothing.
- Remove jewellery; remove or cover rings.
- Always wear serviceable footwear.
- Use correct exercise techniques and keep the weight under control.
- Practise good back-care in the gym – lift correctly and avoid repeated bending.
- Train within your own limitations.
- Never try to train through an injury. If you are injured seek help from a physiotherapist.

Chapter 2

Diet, sport and health

Components of a balanced diet

A balanced diet is essential for the maintenance of good health, and so knowledge of the basic aspects of nutrition complements any weight training programme. In fact, a good training programme without good nutrition is self-defeating. There is an old adage which says 'you are what you eat'; if this is true, then to improve our physique we must also improve our diet.

There are over 50 nutrients which are required in a healthy diet, and these fall into a number of broad groups: carbohydrates, fats, proteins, vitamins, minerals and water. It is a balanced combination of each of these foodstuffs, rather than an excessive consumption of an individual food product, that makes for good nutrition.

Carbohydrates

These are commonly called starches or sugars. They are composed of carbon, hydrogen and oxygen in varying proportions. The basic carbohydrate unit is the monosaccharide, of which the simple sugars glucose, fructose and galactose are examples. Two monosaccharides joined together make a disaccharide, such as sucrose (or table sugar) which is a combination of glucose and fructose. Other disaccharides include lactose (glucose plus galactose), which is found in milk, and maltose (two glucose molecules joined together), which is produced when starch is broken down. When three or more monosaccharide units are joined together they form a polysaccharide. Polysaccharides are used to store glucose for future use as energy. Starch is the polysaccharide found in plants, while glycogen is the polysaccharide used for storage in animals.

A healthy diet is one in which the proportion of refined carbohydrate (monosaccharides and disaccharides) found in sweet foods such as biscuits, chocolate and snacks is reduced, and the proportion of starchy foods containing complex carbohydrates (polysaccharides) such as pasta, potatoes, and grains is increased. In addition to having a high polysaccharide content, foods rich in complex carbohydrates also contain the vitamins and minerals necessary for the body to use the carbohydrate. Foods containing large amounts of refined carbohydrate are highly processed and often contain few vitamins and minerals; they are therefore less nutritious.

Table 1   Carbohydrate-rich foods

Complex carbohydrates (starchy foods – eat more)	Simple sugars (refined foods – eat less)
Wholemeal bread	Sugars, jams, toffee
Brown rice and pasta	Sugary drinks (squashes,
Pulses, beans, peas	lemonade), malted drinks
Potatoes, root vegetables	Jellies, ice cream, sweet
Cereals made from wholegrains	custard
Fresh fruit	

Fats

A fat consists of a glycerol molecule with three fatty acid molecules attached, and is more accurately termed a 'triglyceride'. The type of fatty acid which is present will determine the type of fat. Each fatty acid is a chain of carbon atoms, with a given number of hydrogen atoms attached at specific points. If all these areas are filled with hydrogen atoms, the fat is said to be *saturated* (the sort normally found in animals) and is usually a solid at room temperature. If fewer hydrogen atoms are present, and the fat has a double connection (bond) between two of its molecules, it is *unsaturated* (the type found in vegetable fats and oils) and is normally a liquid at room temperature. *Polyunsaturated* fats have more than one double bond and are found in seeds and fish.

Unfortunately, to confuse the matter, an unsaturated fat can be hardened by a process called *hydrogenation*. It then changes to a 'trans fatty acid', which can be considered the same as a saturated fat. In other words, food may say that it contains vegetable fat, but if this fat has been hydrogenated it is more like animal fat.

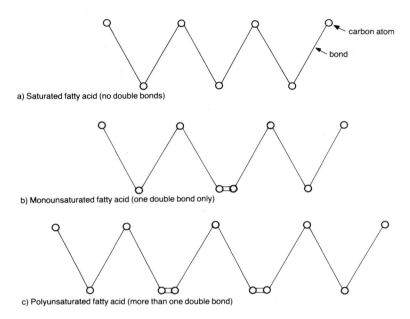

Fig. 1 *Types of fatty acids*

Table 2   Percentage of different fatty acids as a proportion of total fat

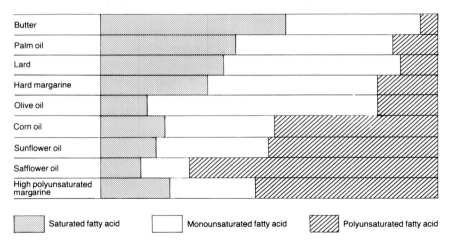

Some fat is essential for good health, so to cut all fat from the diet will starve the body of necessary nutrients and make the diet less palatable. A general recommendation for improved health is to reduce the total amount of fat in the diet, and at the same time to increase the proportion of this fat which comes from vegetable sources (unsaturated or polyunsaturated fat). Table 2 shows the relative proportions of the various fat types commonly found.

Fat should form no more than about 30–35% of the energy intake; of this, saturated fat should make up no more than 10%.

Protein

Proteins are often called the 'building blocks' of the body, but they can also be used as an energy supply in cases of extreme need. Proteins are made up of sub-units called *amino acids*, which contain carbon, hydrogen, oxygen and nitrogen (and sometimes sulphur). There are 21 different amino acids which can combine to form a great variety of proteins. While some amino acids can be exchanged for others, there are eight which cannot be made by the body and so are termed 'essential' amino acids. These must be contained in a balanced diet.

The average daily protein requirement is about 0.8–0.9 g per kilogram body-weight. More is needed in pregnancy and during the adolescent growth spurt, but for adult athletes – even those engaged in bodybuilding activities – the daily requirement is unlikely to be greater than 1–1.5 g/kg body-weight. This is generally provided by the increased amount of food that an athlete consumes, and there is usually no need for protein supplementation. If an excessive amount of protein is eaten it is broken down by the body and the nitrogen portion is excreted in the urine. The amount of nitrogen in the urine can therefore be a good indicator of the amount of protein that an athlete requires.

Both animal and vegetable sources of protein can contain all the essential amino acids. However, in general, vegetable sources do not usually contain all eight essential amino acids, and will be high in some and lower in others. Vegan diets (no meat or animal products) must include a variety of foods to include all the essential amino acids, while vegetarian diets which include eggs and milk products are more easily balanced.

Vitamins

Vitamins perform the chemical reactions which allow the body to function. The body can make certain vitamins, but only in very small amounts; a balanced diet must therefore contain an adequate number and quantity.

Vitamins are designated by both letter and name: for example, vitamin C is ascorbic acid; vitamin B_1 is thiamine. Two vitamin groups exist: those which are soluble in fat (A, D, E, and K), and those which dissolve in water (B and C). Fat-soluble vitamins are stored in body-fat. Daily intake of these vitamins is not necessary because the body's store may last for many years. However, an excessively low-fat diet could in some cases lead to eventual depletion of the fat-soluble vitamins. Similarly, these substances (especially vitamin A) may accumulate to dangerous levels if too many vitamins are taken as supplements. Even the water-soluble vitamins may pose problems if taken in excessive amounts. The major functions of each vitamin are listed in table 3.

Table 3   Vitamins

Vitamin		Good sources	Function(s)
A	Retinol or carotene	Liver, dairy produce, eggs, carrots, green leafy vegetables	Visual processes, connective tissue, skin
B_1	Thiamine	Meat, whole grains, legumes, nuts	Carbohydrate metabolism, CNS function
B_2	Riboflavin	Liver, dairy produce, meat, cereal	Carbohydrate metabolism, vision, skin
B_6	Pyridoxin	Meat, fish, green leafy vegetables, whole grains, legumes	Protein metabolism, red blood cell formation, CNS function
B_{12}	Cyano-cobalamin	Meat, fish, dairy produce; no vegetable sources	Red blood cell formation, CNS function
—	Niacin	Liver, meat, fish, peanuts, cereal products	Carbohydrate and fat metabolism
—	Folic acid	Liver, legumes, green leafy vegetables	Regulates growth of cells, including red blood cells
C	Ascorbic acid	Green leafy vegetables, fruit, potatoes, white bread	Connective tissue, iron absorption/metabolism, healing/infection
D	Calciferols	Dairy produce, action of sunlight on skin	Calcium metabolism, bones and teeth
E	Tocopherols	Vegetable oils, liver, green leafy vegetables, dairy produce, whole grains	Protects vitamins A & C, and fatty acids, from destruction in body (anti-oxidant)
K	—	Green leafy vegetables and liver	Clotting of blood, fat digestion

B vitamins are involved in the metabolic production of energy, so it is often assumed that supplements of vitamin B will in some way improve athletic performance. However, research has not supported this view, and most athletes are better advised to ensure that theirs is a high quality diet rather than seek a 'magic bullet' in the form of a vitamin.

Sometimes vitamin supplementation **may** be called for, in which case a simple multi-vitamin and mineral formulation should be chosen rather than a 'megadose' of a single vitamin. Even then, strict attention should be paid to improving the diet. An athlete on a poor diet who is consuming excessive alcohol may not get enough vitamin B_1, B_{12} or C, and regular large doses of aspirin or anti-inflammatory drugs may reduce the levels of vitamin C. Oral contraceptives may affect the body's stores of folic acid and some B and C vitamins, and smoking can deplete levels of C, B_1 and B_{12}. Athletes such as ballet dancers, jockeys and boxers, who have to diet strictly to get down to a particular competitive weight, may also warrant supplementation if they are unable to take in an adequate number and quantity of vitamins and minerals.

Minerals

About 5% or 8 lb of a 12-stone athlete is composed of a group of 22 elements termed 'minerals'. Minerals are of two main types: *macro* (or major) minerals, which are needed in fairly large quantities (about 100 mg per day); and *trace* elements, which are required in much smaller amounts (2–5 mg per day). As with vitamins, supplementation is not usually required as long as the diet is good. However, in areas where the soil or water supply is poor, mineral deficiency may occur. Of the many minerals which exist (*see* table 4), calcium and iron are especially important to the athlete.

Calcium: This is the most plentiful mineral in the body; combined with phosphorus it forms the bones and the teeth. In addition, calcium plays an essential role in muscle contraction, transmission of nervous impulses, and blood clotting.

Dietary calcium plays a particularly important role in helping to prevent osteoporosis in women after the menopause. Osteoporosis is a condition which involves a progressive decrease in the density of bones. The bones become weaker and are then more susceptible to fractures. Three main factors contribute to the development of this condition: diet; levels of the female hormone oestrogen; and how active a person is. The amount of calcium needed each day can be as high as 1500 mg, but many women consume as little as 300 mg, in some cases placing themselves at risk of calcium depletion. This is especially true in the case of women experiencing

Table 4   Minerals in the diet

Mineral	Sources	Function(s)
Sodium	Salt, cheese, muscle/organ meat, fish/bacon	Neuromuscular transmission (nerve conduction), fluid and acid-base balance
Potassium	Meat, milk, vegetables, cereals, nuts	Neuromuscular transmission (nerve conduction), fluid and acid-base balance
Calcium	Milk, cheese, nuts, green vegetables, bread	Bone/tooth structure, nerve conduction, blood clotting
Magnesium	Green vegetables, meats, dairy produce, cereals	Neuromuscular transmission, bone formation, enzyme reactions – energy metabolism
Phosphorus	Grains and cereals, meat, milk, green vegetables	Bone/tooth formation, energy metabolism
Iron	Nuts/seeds, red muscle/organ meat, eggs, green vegetables	Haemoglobin/myoglobin formation
Zinc	Muscle meats, seafood, green vegetables	Enzyme synthesis
Copper	Shellfish, organ meats, nuts legumes, cocoa/chocolate	Enzyme synthesis
Iodine	Seafood, eggs, dairy produce	Thyroid function
Fluoride	Seafood, water, tea	Tooth structure
Manganese	Nuts, dried fruit, cereals/grains, tea	Enzyme synthesis
Chromium	Meat and dairy products, eggs	Glucose/insulin metabolism
Selenium	Seafood, organ and muscle meats and grains	Anti-oxidant (membranes), electron transfer

the early stages of the menopause. They may require calcium supplements and extra vitamin D under medical supervision.

Iron: Iron is the essential ingredient of *haemoglobin*, the oxygen-carrying compound found in the blood, and of *myoglobin*, an equivalent substance found in muscle. Iron deficiency can therefore lead to marked reductions in performance in endurance events. Those particularly at risk are young women who experience heavy menstrual blood flow, and athletes who need to keep their body-weight unnaturally low. In addition, endurance athletes (who may also fall into one or both of the previous categories) have a larger blood volume, and as a result in some instances may have fewer red blood cells. Intense training leads to iron loss in the sweat and urine, and from gastrointestinal bleeding following long-distance running. General dietary advice for these athletes is to eat iron-rich foods such as liver and whole grains. If anaemia is detected the athlete should receive advice from a dietician.

Salt: The daily salt requirement for the maintenance of health is about half a gram per day, but many people take as much as 12 g. Salt is found in prepared foods and is often added to food during cooking and at the table. Athletes who are eating a large amount of salt should aim to reduce their intake by about half, because a high salt intake can encourage high blood pressure. This in turn can harm the heart. It is in fact the sodium content of the salt which is dangerous, because the delicate balance between sodium and potassium controls blood pressure in the body. It is significant that some people seem less able to tolerate a high salt intake than others; for them it can be especially dangerous.

Fibre

Dietary fibre or 'roughage' is carbohydrate material which is not digested. It is found on the outside of seeds, grains and vegetables. Although fibre is not absorbed by the body it is an essential part of a balanced diet, providing the food with bulk as it passes through the body and helping to remove or 'mop up' waste products in the bowel. This is important for the health of the gut; it is possible that many diseases occurring in developed countries are due in part to food that is too highly refined and contains too little fibre.

Fibrous foods require more chewing than refined foods, and tend to fill you up. They also contain relatively few Calories: for example, if you eat the same number of slices of white and wholemeal bread, the wholemeal will contain fewer Calories because some of its bulk is made up of fibre.

Fibre may be either soluble or insoluble. Soluble fibre is found in foods like peas, beans and oats. Insoluble fibre is contained in cereals and root vegetables. On average, people eat 15–20 g of fibre each day, but for good health this should be increased to about 30 g a day. This fibre should come from a variety of sources such as wholegrain products, cereals, fresh fruit and vegetables. This has the added advantage of increasing the number of vitamins, minerals and trace elements found in the diet. The use of bran tablets is not recommended, because in this concentrated form bran may reduce the levels of calcium, zinc and iron in the body. Some individuals – particularly children and pregnant mothers – already suffer from a deficiency of these minerals, and bran tablets could make this worse.

Fluids and electrolytes

Water is probably the most important single component of the diet. Most of the body's tissues are composed mainly of water, which transports vital substances around the body. Water also plays an important role in temperature regulation. Heat formed by the working tissues during exercise is transported to the body surface and lost to the outside. Sweat is excreted onto the skin and evaporates, cooling the body in the process. During intense exercise, especially on a windy day, fluid loss can be excessive. Athletes training hard in such conditions should drink small amounts of water throughout the training period: large amounts taken in one 'gulp' lead to a bloated feeling and may cause a stitch.

During the fluid-loss process, electrolytes (mainly salt and potassium) are lost. It is thought that this may contribute to muscle cramps, and so many athletes use electrolyte drinks during training. However, it is doubtful whether these are really of benefit, and those containing a lot of sugar or salt should be avoided as they may inhibit fluid absorption. Athletes training regularly in a hot environment should ensure that they eat some salty foods and foods rich in potassium (for example bananas) as a preventive measure.

A note on calories

The energy taken into the body as food and expended during activity is measured in *calories*. One calorie may be defined as the amount of heat required to raise the temperature of one kilogram of water to 1°C. One kilocalorie or Calorie (with a capital 'C') is the more common measure, and this is equivalent to 4.2 Joules, the *joule* being the other measure of food energy.

Carbohydrate, fat and protein can all be used by the body to produce energy, and so may be measured in Calories. Both carbohydrate and protein produce the same amount of energy, one gram of each producing four Calories. Fat is a more concentrated energy source, and one gram of fat can produce nine Calories, more than double the energy of the other two foods. This is why fat is used as an energy store, and reducing it from the diet is a good way to lose weight. Another source of energy, and one that is often overlooked, is alcohol. One gram of alcohol produces eight Calories of energy.

Foods are made up of a mixture of nutrients, and so we give each food a total calorific value which reflects the proportional amounts of the various nutrients it contains. This value is useful to those following a Calorie-controlled diet in order to lose weight, but does **not** reflect the quality of the food. This is because high-calorie foods are not necessarily high in vitamins and minerals, and fibre contains virtually no Calories at all but is still an important part of the everyday diet.

Energy is expended by the body in two ways. Even when 'still' the body requires a certain amount of 'resting energy' for breathing, heartbeat, digestion and other important bodily functions. The amount of energy needed for these processes varies from person to person and depends on many factors, including the size of the body. This resting energy is called the *basal metabolic rate*, and normally uses up about 1200 Calories each day. Energy is also required for 'voluntary activity', including things such as manual work and exercise. People who have very active jobs or who exercise intensely will burn up more Calories than those who tend to be sedentary.

Different sports will burn off Calories at different rates (*see* table 5). For example, slow jogging may use 120 Calories an hour, while driving a car for an hour needs only 48 Calories. Activities during which all the muscles are worked, such as intense swimming or circuit weight-training, can use over 250 Calories in an hour.

Losing weight

When the amount of energy (measured in Calories) from food taken into the body equals the amount being expended during exercise and general metabolic processes, an athlete is said to be in 'energy balance'. In this situation he or she will neither gain nor lose weight. If the energy input is greater than the expenditure, the extra energy will be stored as fat. If too little energy is taken in, the body makes up the deficit by drawing on stored energy and burning up fat.

One method of losing weight is simply to eat less. However, in the case of the athlete this has a number of disadvantages. First, it is more difficult to eat a sufficient quantity of nutrients; and second, tissue other than fat is lost, particularly during extreme reduction diets. When a person begins to diet, they lose mainly water. Initially, 70% of the weight loss is water; this reduces to about 20%

by the time the person has been dieting for about two weeks. Fat loss speeds up as the diet is continued, changing from 25% of the total weight loss in the early days of a diet to about 70% after two weeks. Protein loss increases from 5% to 15% over the same period.

It is not just the amount of food which is important; the type of food eaten is also significant. High-energy foods (those with a lot of Calories, especially fat and alcohol) should be restricted and low-calorie equivalents used. The total amount of food may remain the same. It is important not to reduce the intake of carbohydrate-rich foods too much, as these provide the energy for exercise as well as significant amounts of fibre. It is much better to reduce the quantity of high-fat foods and to follow a low-fat/high-carbohydrate diet.

This diet will be more effective if it is complemented by regular bouts of exercise which increase energy expenditure. The body is such an efficient machine that one period of exercise will not burn up many Calories. However, the increase in metabolic rate that accompanies exercise will continue for some time after the exercise period has finished, so a half-hour work-out will actually continue to burn up Calories for three or four hours after the exercise has been completed. Moreover, provided that the exercise is regular, the small number of Calories which are used will obviously accumulate so that the long-term effect will be quite dramatic. In this way a person may lose 1–2 lb per week safely, without feeling lethargic. The increase in muscle tone which accompanies the weight loss will add greatly to the overall improvement in physical appearance.

The important foods to restrict are alcohol, 'fast' foods such as chips, and snacks like chocolate and crisps, because these are high in fat. Trim all visible fat and grill rather than fry food. Eat wholemeal bread and cereals, and use starchy foods such as potatoes and pasta, rather than sweet things, to give you energy. Remember also that it is body-fat rather than body-weight that is important (see pp. 130–133). Someone starting a weight and fitness programme in combination with a diet will initially lose some weight; however, as their muscles become toned and firm, so their density (and therefore their weight) will increase. Although the amount of body-fat will be considerably reduced, the change in actual body-weight may be less noticeable.

Where a sport requires a particular body-weight, practices such as severe fasting and the use of sweat-suits or diuretics are not to be recommended. Loss of weight through these methods is usually the result of glycogen and water loss rather than the elimination of fat. It is unfortunately not possible to replace water or glycogen in

sufficient amounts immediately prior to competition, so performance almost always suffers.

Gaining weight

Weight gain can be achieved through an increase in body-fat or in
lean body mass, or both. In the case of an increase in lean body
mass, the changes result almost entirely from enlargement of the
muscle fibres through heavy resistance training. Because muscle
tissue is composed partially of protein (it is also largely water),
some athletes assume that taking additional protein will help to
build muscle. This is not the case. Protein recommendations for a
normal individual are 0.8–0.9 grams of protein per kilogram body-
weight. Even the most intensely trained athletes require no more
than 1.0–1.5 grams per kilogram body-weight, and this amount is
easily provided from an increase in food intake. In addition, excess
protein which is not used to make muscle will be burnt up as
energy or stored as fat. The practice of taking large quantities of
milk and eggs to bulk up can in fact be dangerous because it can
raise blood-fat levels.

CHAPTER 3

Energy systems

In order to exercise we need energy, and we get this from the food that we eat. Food is broken down by the digestive system and the nutrients which are released are taken in the bloodstream to the working muscles. Here, the nutrients react with chemical substances called *enzymes* to release the energy that enables us to exercise. Some foodstuffs provide more energy than others. For example, sugars and fats are high energy providers, while fibre is a very low energy source.

When broken down, the energy from the food is stored by special chemicals called *phosphates*. These high-energy phosphate fuels can be thought of as the petrol in the body's engine.

Energy sources

Phosphates are our energy 'currency', and we can 'spend' them in three ways when exercising. This gives us a choice of immediate, short-term, or long-term energy supplies.

Immediate energy sources

A muscle can only store enough phosphate for about 5 seconds of maximal work. The phosphate in this case comes as a special substance called phospho-creatine (PC). This energy source, although used up quickly, is readily available. It enables us to react quickly and work maximally straightaway, rather than waiting for our energy to build up.

For example, it is used in the first few seconds of a sprint and during a low number of maximal repetitions in weight training. It is the energy source for power and speed rather than prolonged strength or endurance activities.

Short-term energy sources (the lactic acid system)

If exercise continues the PC stores will quickly deplete, forcing a muscle to use sugars (glycogen) for energy. This new process is termed *glycolysis*, and enables the muscle to continue to perform intense work – at a price. The price is *lactic acid*, formed as a waste product, which interferes with the working of the muscle. This causes the muscle to ache, and continuing the exercise eventually becomes too painful. The build-up of lactic acid is the source of the 'burn' that is familiar to many sportsmen.

The build-up of lactic acid limits the usefulness of this short-term energy supply to about two minutes. Both glycolysis and the PC system supply energy without using oxygen and are therefore described as *anaerobic*.

Long-term energy sources (the oxygen system)

Long-term energy supplies involve the use of oxygen from the air, and so are termed *aerobic*. Several fuels can be broken down in the presence of oxygen to form energy. These include sugars, fats, and even protein in some cases. As these substances are broken down, their energy is transferred to the body's high-energy phosphates (*see* page 22). This process is slower than both glycolysis and the PC system, and it may be 2–3 minutes before the energy needs of the body cells are met.

During this time the body, which is supplying its tissues with enough oxygen for resting requirements, must take measures to meet their increased needs during exercise. Heart and breathing rates increase; breathing becomes deeper; and the blood flow to the working muscles improves. When all these changes have stabilised, you are said to have reached a 'steady state'.

With training, these changes occur more rapidly because the systems involved become stronger. This is one of the health benefits of regular exercise. People in poor physical condition tend to take longer to reach steady state because their heart, lungs and muscles are not as efficient as those of trained athletes. A comparison between the three energy systems is shown in figure 2.

In practice, the three systems work hand in hand. For example, when you start to exercise, the PC system and glycolysis will supply

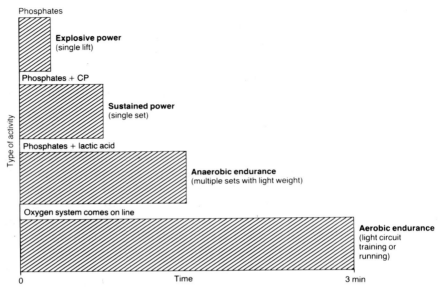

Fig. 2 *Comparison between energy systems*

the energy. The aerobic processes will take slightly longer to come on line. In addition, the aerobic system will not stop immediately on cessation of exercise, but will continue to work for a short while to recharge the other two energy sources. During this period lactic acid and other waste products are removed from the tissues so that they are ready for the next exercise period.

Supplying oxygen to the muscles

To release the energy required for exercise, oxygen from the air is combined with foodstuffs. It is important to understand exactly how this takes place.

Oxygen is taken in by the lungs and carried by the bloodstream to the body cells. In order to understand the changes that occur during exercise it is necessary to look briefly at the various stages of this cycle.

The pulmonary system

We require more oxygen during exercise than we do when we are sedentary; in a vigorous work-out we can increase our need for oxygen by as much as 25 times. In order to get more oxygen we must take in a larger quantity of air. Normally, when we sit quietly relaxing, only a small portion of the lungs is working. Breathing movements are restricted to the upper parts of the lungs, and some of the lung areas are completely shut off.

Air is taken in through the nose and mouth and into the windpipe. This branches into the left and right lung, and then each branch divides again and again into millions of very fine tubes. At the end of each tube a tiny balloon-like airsack fills with air as we breathe in and empties as we breathe out. The airsacks provide a huge surface area; in fact, if they were all flattened out they would cover a whole badminton court! The tubes can be opened or closed by surrounding muscles, and in this way the body can control which areas of the lungs are working at any one time. During an asthma attack these muscles go into spasm, trapping air in the airsacks. If this happens to an athlete who is not used to it, he or she must be told to relax and breathe slowly. If the athlete panics and starts to gasp for air, trying to force the lungs to work, the situation will only get worse.

The lungs are enclosed in the rib-cage, which is a little like a barrel. The floor of the barrel is a sheet of muscle called the *diaphragm*. As we breathe in, two things happen to the chest cavity. First, the diaphragm lowers, pulling the floor of the cavity downwards. Second, the ribs, which are attached to the breast-bone at the front and to the spine at the back, tilt like the handle of a bucket. This pulls them up and out, expanding the walls of the chest cavity. The combination of rib and diaphragm movement increases the size of the chest cavity and pulls air into the lungs. As we breathe out, the process is reversed, and the elasticity of the chest structures and lung airsacks forces air out again (see fig. 3). In heavy smokers the airsacks are less elastic, expansion of the lungs is restricted, and the person therefore finds it difficult to take in sufficient air.

During exercise, additional muscles are used to expand the rib-cage. These accessory muscles of respiration include those of the chest, neck and rib-cage and can be seen working when a person runs flat-out.

The oxygen transport system

Once air has been taken into the airsacks, oxygen moves across the moist airsack walls and into small blood vessels. From here it is taken in the blood to join the nutrients from the food at the working muscle. Carbon dioxide travels the reverse route, from the working muscle in the bloodstream and across the airsack wall. It is then

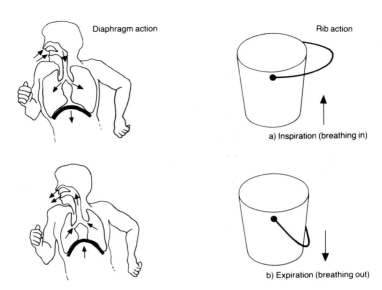

Fig. 3 *Mechanics of breathing*

expelled from the lungs and breathed out.

Oxygen is carried in the blood by a substance called *haemoglobin* contained within the red blood cells. Oxygen-rich blood is red and is carried by the main arteries into smaller blood vessels and capillaries, eventually passing into the body cells themselves. Blood containing carbon dioxide has a blue tinge and is carried in the veins back to the lungs to be breathed back into the atmosphere.

Haemoglobin is rich in iron. People with anaemia have too little haemoglobin and therefore too little iron, and this deficiency impedes their sporting performance. Athletes who train at high altitudes (where the air is 'thinner') have more haemoglobin and red blood cells than others because their body adapts to the lower concentration of available oxygen. This is why athletes competing in countries that are situated at a great distance above sea-level have to spend a period of time before their event training at high altitude. This is known as *acclimatisation*.

With training in general, the body improves its ability to transport and use oxygen for the supply of energy. Fit people therefore have more haemoglobin and a greater number of small blood capillaries in their muscles than unfit people. In addition, their lungs and heart are more powerful so they can get a greater amount of oxygen to their muscles and get it there more quickly.

As we breathe, not all the oxygen is extracted from the air. Room air normally contains about 21% oxygen and a little carbon dioxide. Air which is breathed out still contains about 14% oxygen and 6% carbon dioxide. This is why breathing in a confined space, and so not getting enough oxygen, makes you sleepy. For example, a lot of people having a meeting in a small room with poor ventilation will often feel they cannot concentrate and may have a 'thick head' at the end of the day. Because more oxygen is used during exercise, good ventilation is even more important — windows should be open in the gym!

The cardiovascular system

The heart is really two pumps joined into one. The left side of the heart transports oxygenated blood from the lungs to the working tissues. The right side of the heart takes the blood containing waste carbon dioxide (deoxygenated blood) from the working tissues back to the lungs. The amount of blood pumped by the heart will be determined both by the rate of beating (heart rate or pulse) and by the 'power' of each beat, or the amount of blood that is forced out with each heart-muscle contraction. The blood normally takes approximately 1 minute to circulate around the body, but during exercise (because the strength of each heart beat and the pulse rate are both increased) this time is dramatically reduced, so the same blood will travel around the body up to six times in a minute.

During exercise, then, the heart must beat faster to meet the oxygen requirements of the working body. There is however a limit to how fast it can beat, and the maximum speed reduces with age. You can work out your maximum rate roughly by using the following equation: maximum heart rate = 220 beats/minute − (minus) your age. A 24-year-old would therefore have a theoretical maximum heart rate of 196 beats per minute.

In addition to beating faster during exercise, the heart will also push out more blood each time it beats. The heart is a muscle, and will react to training by getting stronger in the same way as other muscles. A fit individual will have a big, strong heart which is able to pump large volumes of blood. At rest, the heart will not need to pump as quickly, and so the resting heart beat or pulse will be lower. Normally the pulse is about 70 beats per minute; in fit people it can reduce to 60; and in the case of marathon runners it can even go as low as 40 beats per minute because with each beat so much blood is pushed out by the heart.

Another measure of the efficiency of the cardiovascular system is the blood pressure. This is represented by two figures: the first, the *systolic* BP, represents the power of the heart in pushing out blood and will increase during exercise; the second, the *diastolic* BP, reflects the elasticity of the main blood vessels leading from the heart. As the heart pumps blood into these vessels they stretch; as the heart relaxes the vessels spring back. The pressure caused by this elastic recoil is the diastolic BP. This figure will be higher in less fit individuals, as their blood vessels will be more rigid and have less 'give'.

Average blood pressure is 120/80 mm Hg. Blood pressures recorded during isometric work, in which the muscles tense and stay contracted, are higher than those recorded during dynamic work, in which the muscles contract and relax rhythmically. In the case of isometric work, as the resistance to blood flow is increased the muscle contracts and holds, causing a corresponding elevation in blood pressure. During dynamic work, the rhythmic pumping action actually helps the passage of blood through the muscles, and so lower blood pressures are recorded.

CHAPTER 4

How muscles work

If we want to increase strength and body-tone through weight training we are obviously trying to influence muscle. It is therefore important to know how a muscle works. This will enable us to design more effective exercise routines based on science rather than on hearsay.

Muscle fibres

Were we to take a small piece of muscle tissue and magnify it (*see* fig. 4), we would see that it is made up of many long fibres. Each individual muscle fibre is surrounded by a thin membrane. The fibres are grouped in bundles, and the whole muscle structure is encased in a sheath.

A close look at each fibre reveals alternating light and dark bands. The light area is composed of a thin protein filament called *actin*, while the dark area consists of a thicker filament called *myosin*. The two sets of filaments come together like the fingers on two opposing hands (fig. 4(e)). The thin myosin filament has projections coming from it much like the oars of a boat. Further examination of the muscle reveals a network of tiny tubes running into the muscle fibres. These tubes transport chemicals from the outside of the muscle into its centre.

Contraction of the muscle occurs when the muscle filaments move towards each other. When we want a muscle to contract, a nervous impulse is sent from the brain causing changes on the

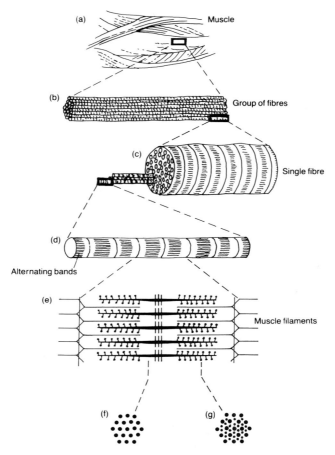

Fig. 4 *Enlarged view of muscle structure*

surface of the muscle fibre. Chemicals travel down the muscle-fibre tubes and into the fibre itself. A chemical reaction occurs which activates the filament projections; these then pull the filaments themselves closer together, causing them to slide over each other and shorten the muscle.

This whole process uses energy, and rest is needed to recharge the contracting structures. Chemicals have to be moved out of the muscle, and the filaments must return to their original relaxed positions.

Not all muscle fibres are of the same type. Some are designed to contract over and over again without fatiguing. These are known as 'slow-twitch' fibres and have a reddish appearance; they are found in the muscles which control posture. Others, which appear white, are called 'fast-twitch' fibres and give short bursts of power such as are required in weight lifting. People have different amounts of these two fibres within a muscle. This is one of the reasons why some individuals naturally excel at a particular sport, while others are never as good, however hard they train.

Strength

How strong a particular muscle is depends on the number and size of the fibres which make it up. The number of fibres is determined at birth, but weight training will make the fibres bigger and therefore make the muscle stronger.

When any muscle fibre contracts, it is only able to reduce in length by half. Although the same amount of shortening occurs in each fibre, altering the arrangement of these fibres within a muscle can affect the muscle's strength. Two different fibrous arrangements are found: one in short, powerful muscles; the other in long, flexible ones.

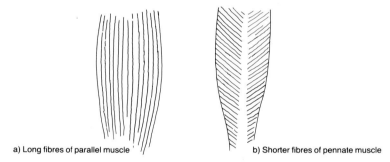

a) Long fibres of parallel muscle   b) Shorter fibres of pennate muscle

Fig. 5 Arrangement of muscle fibres

An example of the short, powerful type is the *deltoid* muscle of the shoulder. In this, the fibres are arranged side by side, inserting into a central tendon like the barbs of a feather. There are many of them, so the muscle is very powerful. However, the fibres are short, so the muscle cannot move very far and is comparatively inflexible. This type of arrangement is called 'pennate', and is illustrated in fig. 5(b).

Long, slender muscles like the hamstrings on the back of the leg have their fibres arranged parallel to each other, attaching to tendons at each end (*see* fig. 5(a)). There are fewer fibres, so the muscle is less powerful than the deltoid. However, the muscle will still shorten by half when it contracts, and as it is much longer the movement it produces will be of a greater range.

When weight training, it is important to be aware of the underlying muscle structure so that you can devise more effective programmes. For example, the hamstrings respond well to fast and explosive plyometric training because they are very long and elastic (see page 81). If heavy weights and slow movements are used to train them they will still get stronger, but are more likely to be injured when subjected to rapid sprinting and lunging movements.

Two other factors are important when talking about strength: the *resting length* of the muscle; and the *speed* of its movement.

A muscle is strongest when it is contracted from a resting (stretched) state (see fig. 6). If the muscle is shortened, less tension can be exerted because an overlap of the muscle filaments interferes with the contraction. If the muscle is overstretched, the filaments are pulled completely apart and no tension can be exerted.

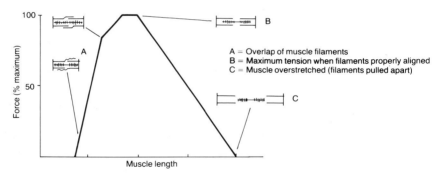

A = Overlap of muscle filaments
B = Maximum tension when filaments properly aligned
C = Muscle overstretched (filaments pulled apart)

Fig. 6 The relationship between muscle length (stretch) and force production

For maximum strength then, we should aim to contract a muscle from a comfortably stretched state. For example, when trying to lift a heavy weight on a bench press, first take the bar right down onto the chest in order to stretch the pectorals. This is more effective than starting from a mid-range position with the bar held off the chest.

There is also a relationship between speed of movement and strength – in fact, there is a trade-off of one for the other. If you lift a very heavy weight you will tend to do so with a slow, strong action using all the muscles fibres. However, when training for a particular sporting action it is important that the speed of an exercise closely matches that of the movement to be carried out in the sport. This is because the changes occurring in the muscle which cause it to become stronger will be specific to the speed of the exercise (*see* page 54).

The group action of muscles

A muscle can only pull; it cannot decide which action to perform. We perform an infinite variety of actions with a finite number of muscles by combining the various actions in different ways. The co-ordinated action of the various muscles responsible for moving a body-part is called the *group action*.

When a muscle pulls to create a movement it is said to be acting as a prime mover or *agonist*. Most muscles can take on this function, depending on the action required and the site of the muscle. The prime mover is often associated with weight training. For example, the biceps muscle of the arm is exercised by performing an arm curl. In this situation, the biceps is the prime mover. In a leg curl, the prime movers are the hamstrings; in a leg extension the prime mover is the quadriceps. However, to restrict ourselves to the use of a muscle merely as a prime mover will greatly reduce the variety of possible exercises and may make our training too specialised.

The muscle which if it contracted would oppose the prime mover is known as the *antagonist*. In the above example we saw that when the biceps contracts to bend the elbow it is acting as a prime mover. To allow this movement to take place the triceps, which would ordinarily straighten the arm, must relax. In this instance the triceps is acting as the antagonist, and its relaxation occurs as a result of an important muscle reflex. This type of muscle action is especially useful when trying to increase the flexibility of a muscle (*see* page 52). For example, if we want to increase the flexibility of the hamstrings, we will get a better stretch by contracting the quadriceps at the same time. This is because the hamstrings in this situation are antagonists to the quadriceps and will therefore relax, allowing us to stretch them that little bit further.

Muscles do not simply create movement; they are also able to stabilise parts of the body or to prevent unwanted actions by acting as 'fixators'. In such cases the muscle will contract to steady or support the bone onto which the prime mover is attached. For example, the deltoid muscle contracts to move the upper arm.

Because this muscle is also attached to the shoulder-blade (scapula), it would tend to move the blade on the back of the rib-cage. To prevent this, muscles running from the spine to the shoulder-blade contract, thus acting as fixators. The fixating action can be very important in cases of injury. Although they are only small muscles, if the scapular fixators are damaged the whole shoulder mechanism is disrupted and the arm cannot work properly.

Many muscles can perform more than one movement. In the case of the biceps, for example, the muscle can twist the forearm upwards (an action known as supination) as well as flex the elbow. If we just want the biceps to perform one action – i.e. to bend the arm but not twist it – other muscles must contract to stop the twisting movement. These muscles, which eliminate unwanted actions, are acting as *neutralisers*. It is important to understand that the biceps muscle cannot 'decide' which action to perform and which not to perform: a muscle can only pull. If we want to prevent it from bringing about an action, other muscles must come into play as neutralisers.

Further muscle actions

As well as the standard actions described above, muscles have a number of other obscure functions. These are less important in the context of weight training, so will be discussed only briefly.

Ballistic contractions

Ballistic actions occur when rapid exercise sequences are performed. Here, the momentum of the moving limb is used to reduce the amount of muscle force required to keep the action going.

For example, when we swing the arm vigorously forwards and backwards when marching or running, muscles contract to propel the arm forwards. Others stop the arm at the end of the movement, and then move it back to its starting position.

Reciprocal contractions

Reciprocal contractions occur when the antagonist is worked immediately prior to the contraction of the agonist. For example, it has been found that greater force is generated from the quadriceps when the knee is bent before it is straightened. This forms the basis of 'pre-stretching', a technique used in bodybuilding and powerlifting.

Two-joint muscles

Some muscles have an effect on two joints. The hamstrings, for example, are able to bend the knee **and** extend the hip, while rectus femoris on the front of the thigh can flex the hip **and** extend the knee.

To prevent these muscles from getting too short and thus losing tension, one end will shorten while the other is stretched so that the overall length of the muscle remains the same. Take as an example the walking action. As the hip is extended the upper part of the hamstrings is shortened; at the same time the knee is extended, so the lower part of the hamstrings is stretched.

Types of muscle contraction

Imagine that you are performing an arm curl. When you bend your arm and lift the weight your biceps muscle is said to be working *concentrically*. A concentric action occurs when a muscle is shortening and so reducing the angle made by the bones of the joint. This is the movement normally associated with weight training; used in isolation, however, concentric contractions will cause imbalances in strength development.

If in the example of the arm curl you hold the weight still, by muscle force alone, the muscle is said to be working *isometrically*. An isometric contraction is produced when there is no change in the external length of the muscle. This type of contraction is used to stabilise a joint and hold it locked in one position. It is also very useful after injury to a joint, because the muscle can be kept strong. Normal exercise might further endanger the damaged joint.

When the weight used in our arm curl is lowered under control, the muscle is lengthening but still producing tension. In such a situation it is said to be acting *eccentrically*. Eccentric contractions are frequently used to resist gravity, the muscles acting as a 'brake' and decelerating the movement. The tension generated is greater than that produced by other contractions, so more weight can be handled. This feature is used to advantage with 'negative reps'.

In the case of the concentric and eccentric muscle actions described above, the speed of movement may vary. As the arm curl is performed, certain parts of the motion can be performed quite quickly, while the part of the movement near the 'sticking point' at the horizontal is likely to be slower. With these two types of contraction the resistance is constant, but the speed of movement will vary depending on how hard you push or pull.

Another type of contraction can occur, during which the speed of movement is kept constant mechanically by constantly changing the resistance. This is called an *isokinetic* contraction, and is very safe because the resistance can never exceed the strength of the muscle. At the moment, machinery allowing this type of training is very expensive and so is limited to medical and research facilities. However, as the price of the machinery comes down we may well see this apparatus more frequently in the gym.

Range of movement

The range of movement (ROM) of a muscle refers to the length of the muscle at any given time. *Outer range* is from a fully stretched position to the mid-point in the movement. *Inner range* is from this point to a fully shortened position of the muscle. *Mid-range* is an area between these two extremes, and is the region in which most everyday movements take place (*see* fig. 7).

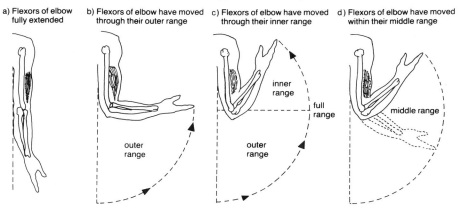

Fig. 7 Range of movement of a muscle

A weight training programme should utilise a joint's full range of movement wherever possible. If it does not, stretching exercises must be incorporated into the routine during the cool-down period to prevent the muscles from shortening and becoming inflexible.

Body movement

Standard terminology can be used to describe the movements of the various parts of the body. For example, bending is called *flexion*; straightening is *extension*; and straightening past the midpoint so that the joint bends back on itself is *hyperextension*. Figure 8 illustrates the most common actions.

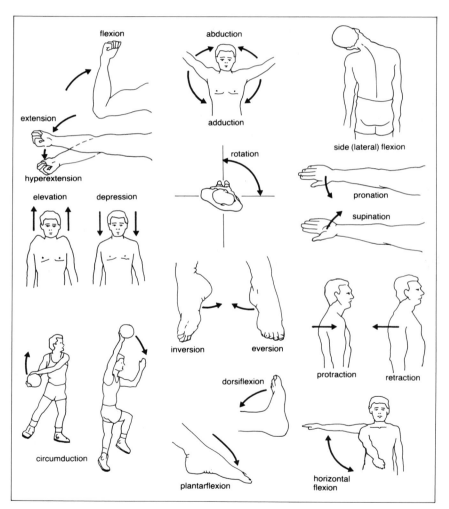

Fig. 8 *Types of movement*

CHAPTER 5

Body shape and composition

Body composition

Body-weight can be a misleading concept. People often talk about being overweight when they really mean 'over-fat', and about being underweight when they actually mean 'under-muscled'. The total weight of the body is the sum of the weight of a variety of tissues, including bone, muscle, fat, fluids and different types of connective tissue. It can be more conveniently divided into body-fat and lean body mass, or the tissue which remains after the fat has been removed.

Body-fat is stored under the skin, around organs, and in bones and nerves. The amount of fat that is desirable can vary, but in general men should have 10–15%, while in women the amount is slightly higher – around 20–25%.

Body-fat is usually assessed by measuring skinfolds (see pp. 131–133). Body-fat measurements are useful, because when a person first starts a weight training programme they usually want to tone up and 'lose weight'. In fact, they will probably lose body-fat, but their weight may initially increase because toned muscle is denser than untoned muscle.

Body type

Each of us has a different type of body. Some are fatter; some are thinner; some are more or less muscled. Each individual's body may be classified as one of three extreme body types: *endomorphs*, *mesomorphs* and *ectomorphs* (see fig. 9).

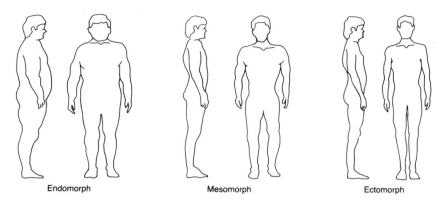

Endomorph   Mesomorph   Ectomorph

Fig. 9 Somatotypes – the three extreme body types

Endomorphs have relatively round physiques and tend to put on and store fat. They have a 'pear drop' appearance, with the abdomen as large or larger than the chest – the typical 'Billy Bunter' character. Mesomorphs have more bone and muscle development. Their bodies are made for strenuous physical activity, and individuals of this type tend to be heavily muscled. The chest is broad, and the shoulders are wider than the waist – the 'Tarzan' type. Ectomorphs have long delicate limbs – the traditional 'bean-poles'.

In reality, few people have a physique which falls firmly into one of these categories. We are all a mixture between the three extremes. By taking height, weight, bone size, limb girth and body-fat measurements, an individual can be given a score indicating the proportion of each type of body component present in their physiques.

Scores range from 1 to 7, and are presented in the order endomorph/ mesomorph/ectomorph. Thus a highly endomorphic individual would score 7/1/1, and a high mesomorph 1/7/1. The somatotype rating can be illustrated graphically so that averages for different sports can be compared (*see* fig. 10). For example, both gymnasts and ice hockey players tend to have a high degree of mesomorphy, but the hockey players are more endomorphic than the gymnasts. Bodybuilders are highly mesomorphic, as one would expect. Swimmers have average scores on all counts, possibly reflecting the fact that these athletes use their own body-weight working against water as resistance.

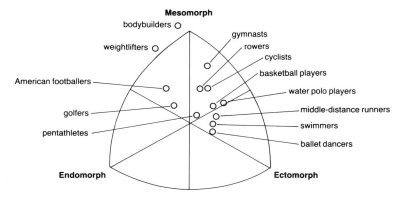

Fig. 10 Elite athlete somatotypes

Body symmetry

When using weight training to strengthen the body, it is essential that *symmetry*, or balance of muscular development, is maintained. For example, if an athlete performs more pushing than pulling activities, the muscles in front of the shoulders will be stronger and usually tighter than those at the back. This can create a round-shouldered posture.

Similarly, there must be a balance between quadriceps and hamstring development at the front and back of the thigh. The strength relative to each other of these two muscle groups can be an important determinant of the state of health of the knee. The weaker muscle of the pair can also be more susceptible to injury.

Other important factors regarding the body's symmetry involve the relationship between strength and flexibility. If a muscle is strengthened through weight training, it will become less flexible and possibly more susceptible to injury. To prevent this from occurring, flexibility training must be incorporated into the exercise programme. Similarly, if a muscle is very flexible but is not correspondingly strong, the joint to which it attaches may become unstable.

Posture

Posture is something which can be greatly affected by weight training. A generally poor posture can be improved, and specific postural faults corrected. On the negative side, an unbalanced training programme can actually create postural problems. Examples include the unequal arm-muscle development of a poorly trained tennis player, and the round-shouldered barrel chest of an inexperienced bodybuilder.

Posture is maintained both by muscles and by non-contractile tissues; a good posture is one which places the least possible stress on both. A good posture requires little muscle activity, so it is more relaxed and needs less energy to maintain it. At the same time, joint structures are not overstretched or shortened so much that they cause strain. In both of these cases a good posture is one which is balanced.

Two types of posture are important. *Static* posture is the body position of a person who is at rest, while *dynamic* posture is the type of body position that a person takes up when moving. In this text we will limit ourselves to static posture, because an analysis of dynamic posture normally requires complex analysis using video equipment and computers to 'freeze' the action.

A number of factors interact to create a person's static posture. Somatotype (*see* pp. 39–40) and genetic make-up are both important. So too are strength and flexibility, as well as the way in which you look at yourself – your 'self-image' and your mental state.

On the whole you cannot alter your skeletal structure, so the posture with which you were genetically endowed is permanent (unless you have it surgically altered – children with specific spinal deformities often require a number of complex operations to straighten the spine, for example). Similarly, if you have large or small bones you are stuck with them. You should plan your training programme to take into account your particular body shape.

In the case of both strength and flexibility the important factor is symmetry. An unequal development of either can pull the body out of alignment and so cause postural faults. If a poor posture is being caused by a tight tissue or a weak muscle, exercises can be performed under the direction of a physiotherapist to correct the fault or faults – sometimes with quite startling results.

Finally, a person's mental state must be considered. If someone is depressed, they tend to be more round shouldered and flat chested as though the world's problems are pressing them down: a general lack of confidence, particularly in the case of children, can have similar effects. The combination of improved confidence and self-image and the general increase in strength which can result from a weight training programme often transforms a teenager's posture so that he 'walks tall with pride'.

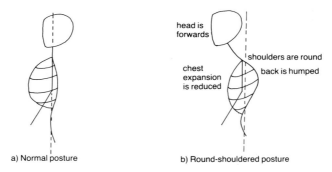

a) Normal posture   b) Round-shouldered posture

Fig. 11 *Showing normal and faulty posture*

Common postural faults

Lower back

The lower part of the back, the *lumbar spine*, should normally be slightly hollow. This curve (the *lumbar lordosis*) is greatly affected by the tilt of the pelvis. The pelvis is balanced like a see-saw on the hip joints, and is controlled by the abdominal, spinal and hip muscles and by the ligaments which surround these areas. The abdominal muscles and the hamstrings will tilt the pelvis backwards and flatten the lower spine, while the hip flexors and spinal extensors will tilt the pelvis forwards and increase the lumbar curve (*see* fig. 12).

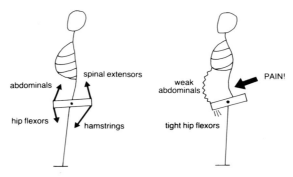

Fig. 12 *Control of the pelvic tilt*

Weak abdominal muscles or tight hip flexors often allow the pelvis to drop and tilt too far, increasing the lumbar curve. Strengthening the abdominals and stretching the hip flexors will go some way towards normalising the lumbar curve and can greatly reduce back-pain.

In cases where the lumbar curve is too flat, especially after prolonged periods of back-pain, exercise can help to restore the curve. A simple exercise can be performed by lying on the floor, keeping the hips down, and pushing up with the arms (see fig. 13). Over a period of time the arms can be straightened more and more until the spine bends normally. However, if this movement causes pain the person should perform spinal exercises under the supervision of a physiotherapist.

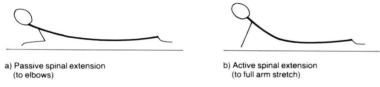

a) Passive spinal extension
(to elbows)

b) Active spinal extension
(to full arm stretch)

Fig. 13 Restoring the lumbar curve

Head, neck and shoulders

The common fault in this area is a round-shouldered posture (see fig. 11). This has the 'knock-on' effect of allowing the head to protrude too far forwards (poking chin), and causing the upper spine to hump. This humped spinal posture in turn forces the ribs together and restricts chest expansion. To prevent this fault, or to correct it in its early stages, exercises which pull the shoulders back – such as seated rowing – are used. If the problem has been present for some time the chest muscles may have tightened, as may the tissues on the back of the neck. To stretch these structures out, exercises which pull on the chest, such as the 'vertical flye' (pec deck) and 'dumb-bell flye', should be chosen, and performed using very light weights. In addition, pulling in the chin will stretch the structures on the back of the neck (see fig. 14). Remember that tight structures take time to stretch, so the movements must be performed in a slow, controlled fashion. The aim is to encourage, rather than to force, the movement.

When viewed from behind, the neck and shoulders can also be seen to be pulled out of alignment. One shoulder is often higher

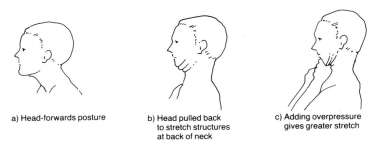

a) Head-forwards posture   b) Head pulled back   c) Adding overpressure
to stretch structures   gives greater stretch
at back of neck

Fig. 14 Correction of faulty neck posture

than the other, and the neck may be tilted. These distortions usually arise from muscle imbalances or from tight muscles, tendons and ligaments. If tightness is the cause gentle stretching should alleviate the condition. Balanced muscle strength can be restored through a carefully designed weight training programme. Athletes who use only one arm in their sport, such as javelin throwers and tennis players, often suffer from poor alignment in the head, neck and shoulder area.

Lower limb

Postural faults in the foot and leg can affect the efficient functioning of the knee joint. Weight training can help to correct some of them. If the foot flattens too much (*pronates*) this places an unnatural stress on the foot and knee structures, and will almost certainly cause pain. This can be particularly noticeable when a person performs a squat (*see* fig. 15). If this is done in bare feet, or in a shoe which is too soft, the foot will flatten excessively along its inner edge. This in turn will cause the shin bones to twist and pull the knees inward into a 'knock-kneed' position. Constant repetition of this action will stress the foot, shin and inner side of the knee. To prevent this, wear good shoes which support the foot and practise good exercise technique.

A common problem in sport is pain at the front of the knee, beneath the kneecap. One of the causes of this is an imbalance between the different components of the quadriceps muscles. Normally the kneecap travels in a shallow groove on the front of the thigh bone (*femur*). However, if the inner quadriceps muscle (*vastus medialis*) is weak, or the outer knee structures are tight, the kneecap can be pulled outwards too far. This unnatural movement can cause the lower edge of the kneecap to rub on the bone beneath, producing

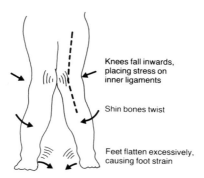

Knees fall inwards,
placing stress on
inner ligaments

Shin bones twist

Feet flatten excessively,
causing foot strain

Fig. 15 *Pronation and knock-kneed position when squatting*

inflammation and pain. Management of this condition involves specialised physiotherapy, but one of the mainstays of treatment is to strengthen the inner quadriceps with weight training using a modified leg extension and quarter-squat exercise.

Postural examination

When planning a training programme it is a good idea to work with a partner and to examine each other's posture to see if there are any faults which could be corrected by a well-planned schedule. Standing posture can be assessed from the side and from behind, by comparing parts of the body with a horizontal and vertical line (*see* fig. 16). Record which side of the body is showing the fault, and compare your chart every six months to determine progress.

Sex differences and weight training

Women often hesitate to begin a weight training programme for fear of becoming too muscular. However, scientific studies have shown that both men and women show similar gains in strength relative to their body-weight.

Between the two sexes, the main difference in response to weight training is the increase in muscle size (*hypertrophy*) which usually occurs. Although strength gains in proportion to body-weight are similar, changes in muscle girth measurements are substantially less for women than for men. This may be due to hormonal differences between the sexes. Testosterone is a powerful tissue-building hormone; men have 20–30 times more of this hormone

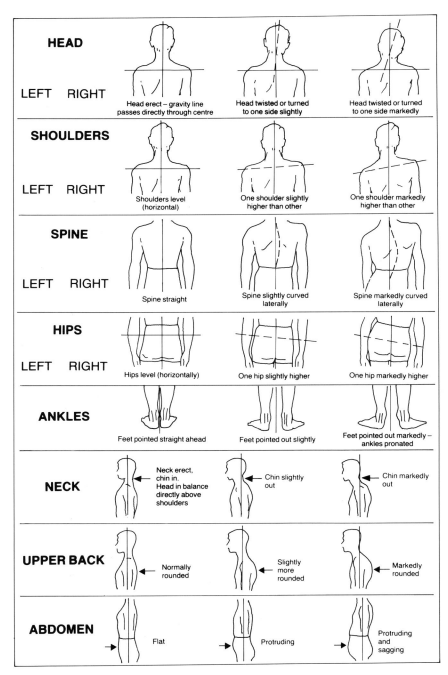

Fig. 16 Posture check-list

than women, and therefore put on more muscle mass when they do heavy weight training.

The precise amounts of hormones will vary between individuals. Some women will have more testosterone than is average, and some men will have less. This is why certain women develop thicker muscles than they would like, and some men find it difficult to build muscle mass, however hard they train.

Exercise during pregnancy

As the female body changes during pregnancy, so the appropriate amount and type of exercise will change. Most women will gain 20–35 lb during pregnancy: their centre of gravity and thus their posture will alter. The pelvic tilt increases; the centre of gravity moves forwards; and so, to compensate, the lumbar curve is accentuated. Increased breast mass during later pregnancy causes the hump of the upper back (*thoracic kyphosis*) to get larger, and the head is then held in a protruded position. In addition to these compensations for altered weight distribution, hormones are released to relax the pelvic ligaments and so aid childbirth. However, the effect of the hormones is not just restricted to the pelvic tissues, and all ligaments will become more lax making the joints susceptible to overstretch.

The combination of altered spinal mechanics and relaxation of ligaments often gives rise to pain in the lower back during the later stages of pregnancy. Strength training, provided it is applied with caution, can ease this discomfort by maintaining muscle strength and therefore joint support.

Changes in body composition also occur during pregnancy. There is an increase in fluid retention, metabolic rate, body-heat and waste production. These changes are compounded by intense training, which can cause excessive heat gain and reduce the amount of blood flowing to the foetus. Both of these factors reduce the amount of oxygen reaching the child. For these reasons, athletes should train at an intensity slightly below that which they are generally used to, and avoid highly intense exercise altogether during the later stages of pregnancy.

Certain positions, particularly lying on the back (supine lying), can interfere with the return of blood to the heart, so exercises such as sit-ups, which require the athlete to remain supine for long periods, should be avoided. Dizziness can be brought on by changing the body position too rapidly, so the athlete should be prepared for this and rest quietly should it occur.

Research has shown that a number of benefits can be reaped from controlled exercise during pregnancy. The duration of labour is less, and labour is generally easier. The likelihood of needing a Caesarean section is reduced, and the average length of hospitalisation is less. Women who exercise regularly also recover more quickly from childbirth. As a general rule, follow these guidelines.

- Do not suddenly increase the amount of exercise done.
- Avoid high-risk exercises, such as water skiing, contact sports and skin diving.
- Avoid highly intense, exhausting exercises.
- Do not hold the breath while exercising or practise the valsalva manoeuvre.
- Always perform a thorough warm-up and cool-down.
- Monitor heart rate and stay well within the recommended limits.
- Drink regularly while exercising.
- Avoid exercises lying on the back on the floor.
- Avoid high-impact activities.
- Do not change position suddenly, as this may cause dizziness.
- Wear supporting/shock-absorbing shoes and choose a bra which gives good breast support.
- Practise good nutrition throughout pregnancy.
- Avoid excessive flexibility exercises because of joint laxity during late-stage pregnancy.

Weight training for children

The physical and psychological benefits of weight training make it a desirable pastime for young people, but several precautions must be exercised when training pre-adolescents. In this age-group, fractures can occur across the cartilage end-plate of the bones, and have been reported as a result of overhead weight-lifting activities. Similarly, the soft-tissue injuries which are commonplace in sport can occur during or as a result of weight training. The cause of most injuries is incorrect technique, which places unnatural stresses on the body. Correct technique is therefore of paramount importance in weight training, and especially in youngsters.

Increases in blood pressure with resultant black-out have been noted with the 'valsalva' manoeuvre, in which a deep breath is taken and forcibly held. This technique is not generally to be recommended in the case of inexperienced users. It should never be allowed in the young. In addition, when teaching correct weight training technique to youngsters it is important to ensure that they breathe properly. 'Breathe out on effort' is a good maxim, and it should be enforced from day one.

One of the features of weight training is that it allows an athlete to isolate individual parts of the body and particular actions, and to improve musculature and performance accordingly. This can however create a programme which is too specialised for the young, and pre-adolescent weight training programmes must be planned as part of a general fitness regime so that a proper balance can be maintained. The young require a wide repertoire of skills, which in turn requires a variety of physical training. For them, increases in weight should be seen as considerably less important than a correct technique.

Weight training in the elderly

Weight training has traditionally been seen as a sport for young, fit athletes. However, resistance training of all types is used in rehabilitation programmes for hospital patients, so it is easily applied at lower intensities.

The elderly can benefit from properly designed and supervised weight training regimes, especially circuit training. Increases in strength, mobility and cardio-pulmonary fitness can be achieved even in later life. As is the case with the young, weight training for the elderly should be applied as part of a general fitness programme to provide a good variety of exercise components.

Before starting a weight training programme, an elderly individual should undergo a medical examination, and his or her musculoskeletal system should be assessed by a physiotherapist. This latter precaution is partly to reduce the likelihood of musculoskeletal injury, but also because a number of medical conditions encountered in the elderly respond extremely well when a short period of rehabilitation is performed before a general weight training programme is started.

CHAPTER 6

The components of fitness

What is fitness? Is a delicate ballet dancer 'fit' to play in a rugby scrum, or a sumo wrestler 'fit' to run marathons? Common sense tells us that these athletes would not be considered suitable for the alternative sports suggested, and yet most would agree that both top-class ballet dancers and wrestlers are fit.

The answer to this conundrum is that two types of fitness exist: that which is necessary for general health (*health-related fitness*); and the extreme requirements for excellence at a particular sport or activity (*task-related fitness*).

In the case of general health, three things are vital: stamina, suppleness and strength.

Health-related fitness

Stamina

Stamina relates to the condition of the heart, lungs and circulation. It describes the ability to keep doing a particular exercise without getting breathless. Exercises that improve stamina are rhythmical in nature; examples include fast walking, swimming, and cycling, all of which make the heart beat faster and keep it at this rate for some time.

This type of exercise strengthens the heart muscle, expands the lungs and conditions the blood vessels, and it is these changes which help to protect an individual from heart problems.

When training to improve stamina, three factors are important: how hard an exercise is (intensity); how long it goes on (duration); and how often it is performed (frequency). The intensity of an exercise can be assessed by measuring the heart rate. The maximum heart rate (HRmax) is generally said to be (220 − age) beats/min (*see* page 27). In order to gain the benefits of stamina training, the heart rate must increase to what is known as the *target heart rate* (THR); this is a percentage of the age-determined maximum.

There is a trade-off between intensity and duration of exercise. Generally speaking, the harder an exercise is, the less you need to do of it; there are however upper and lower limits of intensity, duration and frequency of training. On average, three periods of stamina work are required each week, at an intensity of between 70% and 90% of HRmax. The lower percentage is more suitable for beginners, and exercise of this intensity should be continued for about 30–40 minutes. Higher intensities will suit the more experienced athletes, and need only be carried out for 20–30 minutes. If a person simply runs 'flat out' for 2 minutes the intensity of the exercise is sufficient, but the exercise will not have been kept up for long enough to allow the necessary changes to occur in the body. Similarly, a casual stroll around the park may be of a sufficient duration, but the exercise intensity is too low.

It is also important to realise that the duration of the stamina training refers only to the aggregate of the times at which the heartbeat is high. It does not refer to the duration of the work-out itself. You may spend 40 minutes in the gym, but possibly half of this time is spent resting or waiting for apparatus to become free. The heart rate will reduce in these periods and they will not count towards improving your stamina.

Suppleness

This refers to the amount of movement at a joint, and is an important factor in determining its health. Suppleness exercises are slow and controlled. They move a joint through its full range of motion so you feel the 'stretch'.

Three types of stretching are generally used: *static*, *ballistic* and *neuromuscular*. Static stretching is the type used in yoga. The fully stretched position is held, and any tightness gradually subsides. Ballistic stretching is often used in sport and involves adding small 'bounces' when at the fully stretched position in an attempt to extend the range of movement still further. This method of stretching is very dangerous and cannot be recommended; the rapid movements trigger a reflex response that actually tightens the muscle you are trying to stretch. If the stretch is very vigorous and a lot of momentum is built up, the non-contractile joint structures themselves, especially the ligaments, may give way. These structures are essential to the health of the joint; if they are overstretched the joint will be left relatively unprotected.

The third type of stretching, termed neuromuscular, again uses the muscle reflexes, but this time to advantage. When the prime mover muscle contracts, its neighbour, the antagonist, relaxes (see pp. 33–34). This process is used in neuromuscular stretching. For example, if we want to stretch the hamstrings, a simultaneous contraction of the opposing muscle group (the quadriceps) will cause the hamstrings to relax slightly, allowing the stretch to be taken slightly further.

When a part of the body is stretched, then, two types of tissue are affected: contractile tissue (muscle); and non-contractile tissue (ligaments, tendons, joint capsules, etc.). Normally it will be the muscles that limit the movement, and so neuromuscular or static stretching is used. After injury, however, the non-contractile structures may tighten. When stretching these, basic mechanical principles apply – the tissue will become more pliable when heated. This may be partially achieved through an active or passive warm-up. When stretching a tight ligament or joint capsule after an injury, a physiotherapist may use a form of heating called shortwave diathermy to convey heat deep into the joint and so make stretching the previously injured tissues much easier. The principles of tissue warming are the same; only the method has changed.

Strength

Strength is important to the integrity of a joint, tightening and also toning muscles. To strengthen a muscle we must work it harder than normal, a process known as overloading. This can be achieved in a number of ways such as doing heavy manual work, working with tension springs, and training with weights. In each case the muscle contracts against a resistance. If the resistance is fairly high, the muscle has to work significantly harder than normal and so strength will develop. If the resistance is lower, strength will still be developed, but normally less effectively. However, a higher number of repetitions can be performed with a lower resistance, so the endurance of the muscle will also be improved.

As a result of strength training two types of change occur in the body. First, there are the changes occurring in the muscle itself.

Individual muscle fibres enlarge as more muscle protein is laid down, and so the muscle itself gets larger, thicker and firmer. In addition, the structural framework which surrounds the muscle enlarges and the muscle develops more blood vessels.

The second type of change involves the nervous control of the muscle, which will also improve allowing more muscle fibres to be used more effectively at any one time. The nervous changes are responsible for the rapid improvements in strength which occur when a person first starts weight training. Initially their muscle size may stay the same, but they will be able to use muscle more efficiently and so lift more weight.

Because the skills involved in different exercises vary, we should really preface the term 'strength' with its relevant 'type' – for example 'isometric strength', or 'concentric strength'. This is important when assessing strength development as a measure of fitness. If we don't define the type of strength used in an action we may not be able to replicate the strength test. For example, a person lifts a 200 lb bench press: how did he do it? Did he lift it slowly or quickly? Did he lift the weight up (concentric strength) and lower it down in a controlled manner (eccentric strength)? To repeat the test accurately we must know these precise details.

Task-related fitness

In addition to general fitness, sports performance requires 'task-related' fitness components, particularly speed, power, skill and specificity. These are not related to general health in the same way as stamina, suppleness and strength. They are however important in the prevention of sports injuries and the safe return to sport after injury.

Speed and power

Speed and power are trained through fast, explosive actions. When a movement is performed quickly, for example a rapid running action, we are developing speed. If a fast action is performed against a resistance, for example a piece of weight training apparatus, we are training for power.

Fast actions build up a lot of momentum, and are therefore difficult to stop. This is an important safety consideration in the case of power training, and power exercises must always be controlled and executed with good technique. Athletes training for power frequently 'pre-stretch' a muscle (i.e. stretch it immediately before contracting it); in this way they utilise the elastic properties of the muscle to overcome a greater resistance. This is the basis of *plyometric* training (*see* pp. 81–82).

Skill

Skill involves a number of components, especially balance and co-ordination. Certain skills will be a blend of inborn and acquired abilities, so their improvement may be limited to some extent.

A skill must be 'refined' if it is to be improved. It is not enough just to practise a particular action over and over again; the action must be corrected, and any awkwardness removed, until finally a smooth, 'grooved' motion is achieved. For example, an athlete wishing to improve his tennis serve cannot simply practise the same technique repeatedly. If he does, he is merely compounding the fault or faults. Coaching is needed to highlight the faulty part of the action, so that it can be corrected and the serve refined.

Skills do not just exist in competitive sport, however; weight training exercises are skills in themselves. In an exercise such as the squat it is a good idea to get some coaching to ensure that you are practising the right movement from the start. If not, you will simply practise incorrect (and sometimes dangerous) actions which are very difficult to correct later on.

Specificity

There are really two aspects to this component. In terms of exercise physiology, specificity refers to the 'SAID' principle, standing for 'Specific Adaptation to Imposed Demand'. This really means that the changes which take place in the body (the adaptation) are very closely related, or specific, to the exercise we use (the imposed demand). For example, an isometric exercise for the arm will develop the greatest amount of strength with the arm joint in a right-angled position. If we were to measure the arm strength with the elbow held at positions of more or less than a right-angle, we would find the strength gain to be inferior. This holds true for fitness components other than strength. Although running marathons and doing sprint training will both make you fitter, the changes that take place within the body will be completely different in each case.

The other meaning of the term 'specificity' encompasses those fitness components which are unique to a sport but may not necessarily be good for the sportsman's health. For example, a high body-weight is important in sumo wrestling; a high degree of flexibility can be required in certain types of ballet and in gymnastics. Athletes wishing to excel at these particular sports will require these specific fitness components, but clearly neither excessive body-weight nor excessive flexibility are good for a person's health.

If you are using weight training to enhance your performance at a particular sport, it is important that you take some time to work out the specific aspects of fitness that your sport demands. Developing the wrong ones will not just waste your time, but may also lower your performance standard!

CHAPTER 7

The mechanics of movement

Mechanics is the study of the laws governing movement. Mechanical principles apply not only to machines, such as cars, but also to the human body and to apparatus in the gym. Looking at a few fundamental principles in this area will enable us to understand more fully some of the science behind good training technique.

In all gyms there are mechanical objects such as levers and pulleys, and in your work-out you will come across mechanical forces which include friction, inertia and momentum. Let's take a look at the principles which govern all of these factors.

Leverage

Leverage occurs when a rigid bar (the lever) turns on a fixed point (the fulcrum or pivot). Many everyday objects involve the use of levers. The hinges of a door act as a fulcrum, while the door itself is a lever. A can opener is a lever, as is a car jack. Whenever a weight is lifted during weight training, part of your body will act as a lever (see fig. 17).

We need to consider two forces when dealing with leverage: *resistance* and *effort*. Effort attempts to create a movement; resistance tries to stop it. In weight training, the weight is the resistance and muscle strength is the effort.

The amount of leverage produced can be calculated by multiplying the resistance by the horizontal distance between the resistance and the fulcrum (it is important that the **horizontal** distance is used,

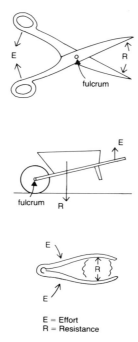

E = Effort
R = Resistance

Fig. 17 *Examples of levers*

and not simply the distance between a weight and the fulcrum).
The further away from the fulcrum a weight is held, the larger the
leverage forces produced.

Fig. 18 shows a simple lever. A resistance of 6 kg is placed 3 m
away from the fulcrum. Multiplying these together gives a leverage
force of 18 units. To balance this out, the effort has to be of the same
magnitude. The 9 kg weight has therefore to be placed 2 m from the
fulcrum for the lever to balance.

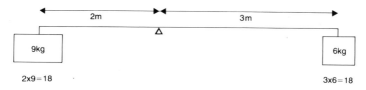

Fig. 18 *Calculating leverage*

In the gym we need to be aware of the concept of leverage. A good
example of this is offered by the arm curl. As the forearm approaches
the half-way point, the leverage is greatest nearest the horizontal. It

reduces as the arm nears the vertical. When using free weights, leverage must always be considered; similar exercises performed with the same amount of weight but with different leverages will require very different amounts of effort.

Take as another example the dumb-bell lateral raise (*see* fig. 19). Here, a dumb-bell is held in the hand and lifted out sideways. Because leverage is calculated using the horizontal distance between the weight and fulcrum, the leverage at the start of the exercise is minimal (the arm is held vertically at the side of the body). As the dumb-bell is raised, the leverage forces increase, reaching a maximum when the arm is held horizontally. Past this point, as the arm is raised above shoulder level, the leverage reduces again and the exercise gets easier.

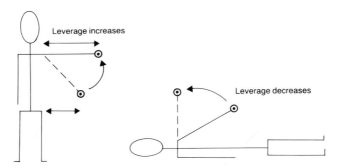

Fig. 19 Leverage in weight training

A similar exercise, using the same weight but performed lying on the side, exhibits very different leverage characteristics. This time the leverage is greatest at the start of the exercise and reduces as the dumb-bell is lifted towards the vertical. As it moves further into an overhead position the leverage again increases.

Leverage is an important factor when trying to prevent injury to the spine. Because the spine is a long column, leverage forces will increase the amount of force necessary to lift a weight. This force will act close to the fulcrum, which in the case of the spine is the hip. The structure closest to the fulcrum in this case is the lumbar (lower) spine, and this is why low back-pain is so common. If a weight is lifted and held close into the chest, the leverage forces are minimal (*see* fig. 20). If the weight is held at arm's length, the leverage forces multiply the effect of the weight by as much as ten times. This will obviously increase the muscular strain on the shoulder, but is also likely to pull the spine forwards, eventually causing back-pain.

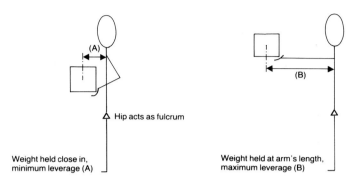

Fig. 20 *Leverage forces acting on the spine*

Various exercises involve potential dangers from leverage, most particularly the squat. When this exercise is performed with the spine upright and vertical a small amount of leverage is created. This is equivalent to the horizontal distance from the fulcrum to the weight, (A) in fig. 21. The weight is held on the shoulders, and the fulcrum is the hip; the leverage is therefore minimal because the horizontal distance between these two points is so small. However, if the spine is allowed to flex, the horizontal distance between the weight and the hip increases, (B) in fig. 21, and so the leverage force is increased. A squat performed with the spine flexed is therefore potentially much more likely to cause injury to the spine.

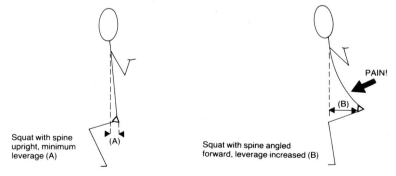

Fig. 21 *Leverage in the squat*

Reducing the length of the lever can make free exercises easier. Take as an example the bilateral straight leg raise (see fig. 22). The leverage is greater when the leg is straight (A) than when the leg is bent (B). Bending the leg thus reduces the strain placed on the spine.

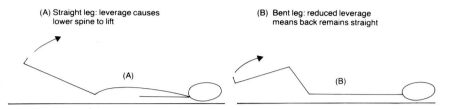

Fig. 22 *Leverage can be dangerous*

Centre of gravity

The centre of gravity of an object is its balance point, or the point at which all the weight of the object is focused. In an 'even' object, such as a brick or a weight disc, the centre of gravity is at its centre; in 'uneven' objects, such as the human body, the centre of gravity is nearer to the larger, heavier end.

When a person is standing, their centre of gravity lies within the pelvis. This point will change as the body position changes, and, as the centre of gravity is partially determined by the weight of an object, will move when something is carried.

Stability

Stability is important in the gym primarily for injury prevention. When lifting a weight, an unstable position is a dangerous position, particularly at the end of a work-out when fatigue is setting in.

When discussing stability there are two factors to consider. First, the position of the 'object's' centre of gravity; and second, the size of the 'object's' supporting base. An object with a low centre of gravity and a wide supporting base is likely to be stable.

Take as an example a motorbike. It has narrow wheels and therefore has a small base of support. In addition, the rider sits on the machine and so his centre of gravity is high. In contrast, a racing car has a wide base of support, and the driver sits low in the car rather than on top of it so the centre of gravity is low. The driver's position and the vehicle itself are thus more stable.

The same principles can be applied to situations in the gymnasium. When using exercises above head height, such as shoulder pressing actions and lateral dumb-bell raises, the lifter has a high centre of gravity and so is less stable. Taking a wide stance will help to compensate for this. Similarly, in squatting exercises a wide stance should be used, with the toes turned out to maximise the base of support.

Many exercises are more stable when performed in the seated position, because the body's centre of gravity is lower. For example, if shoulder exercises are performed seated, the athlete is more stable and less body sway occurs.

To increase stability, then, the base of support must be as wide as possible and the centre of gravity as low as possible. In addition, the centre of gravity should be well within the base of support to allow for minor movements.

When the lifter is moving, the base of support should be widened in the direction of the movement. In the case of a pulling action, a wide stance should be taken with one foot in front of the other; during a dumb-bell lateral raise the feet should be astride.

Adopting these more stable positions when you are first introduced to training will make them second nature in a very short time. The result is that your safety while training will improve accordingly.

Momentum, inertia and friction

These are all forces which work upon the weight that you are lifting, making it harder or easier to move.

Inertia

Inertia is an object's resistance to changes in movement, and is proportional to its weight or 'mass'. The heavier an object is, the more inertia it will have; thus a car is hard to push, and a bicycle relatively easy.

Inertia is important when lifting a heavy weight. It will be difficult to get the weight moving, but once it is on the move less force is needed to keep it going.

Friction

Friction is the force which tries to stop one object from sliding over another. Frictional forces are produced by roughness on the surfaces of two opposing objects; if the objects are lubricated (using oil, for example), the friction will be reduced. In weight training, friction is an important factor in the use of pulley wheels. When a weight is being lifted on a pulley, both the weight of the object and the frictional forces between the pulley wheel and cord must be taken into account. Different machines may give very different resistances – even if the same weight is being lifted – if their frictional forces vary.

Momentum

Momentum is a combination of how heavy an object is (its *mass*) and how quickly it is moving (its *velocity*). Heavy weights moving quickly will possess a lot of momentum, and can be dangerous if they are not handled correctly.

There is a high risk of a weight with a lot of momentum taking over the movement; instead of being lifted in a controlled fashion it can pull the lifter. This is when injuries can occur. To reduce the effect of momentum, weights should be slowed down and lowered in a controlled fashion at the end of each movement. If this is not done, the momentum still present in the moving limb and weight may tear at a joint and cause injury.

Pulleys

A pulley is simply a wheel mounted on an axle. In the case of a single fixed pulley the force exerted along the rope is the same at all points (*see* fig. 23).

Fixed pulleys are used to change the direction of a force. For example, a vertical pull in weight training can be changed into a horizontal pull, enabling a rowing action to be performed with an upright weight stack.

Moveable pulleys involve different leverage forces from the standard, fixed type. The edge of the pulley on the trailing rope acts as the fulcrum (*see* fig. 24), and the resistance comes between the fulcrum and the effort.

The leverage of the effort is twice that of the resistance, and so the actual force exerted to raise the pulley will only be half the amount marked on the weight. This can be particularly useful in the context of rehabilitation.

Another method of altering the resistance is to change the shape of the pulley, so that it is not round but asymmetrical. This type of pulley is called a 'cam', and is designed to vary the resistance offered to a muscle throughout a movement. In fig. 25(A) the resistance arm is slightly larger than that of the effort, and this would be used at limb positions where the muscle is strong. In fig. 25(B) the cam has

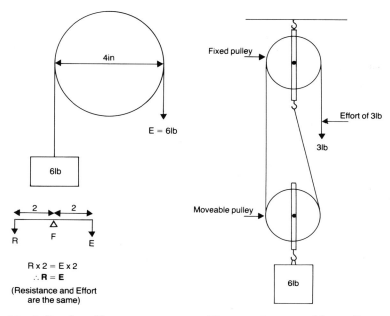

Fig. 23 A fixed pulley   Fig. 24 A moveable pulley

rotated, so that the resistance arm is now considerably shorter and the weight is easier to lift. This cam position should correspond to the weakest part of the movement, or the 'sticking point'.

As a muscle contracts, the resistance which it can overcome will vary depending on a number of factors, for example limb length, muscle type and length, starting position and leverage. Different cams can therefore be designed for specific parts of the body.

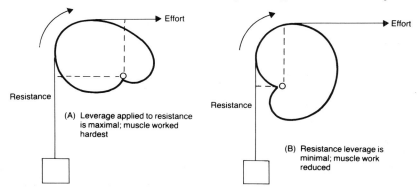

Fig. 25 Variable resistance using a cam

CHAPTER 8

Weight training apparatus

To increase the strength or tone of a muscle we need to make it work harder than it normally would in everyday life – i.e. to 'overload' it. There are many different ways in which this can be done: weight training, the use of springs and rubber bands, and exercising against water are just a few examples.

This section will describe the various types of weight training apparatus, and discuss the advantages and disadvantages of each.

Free weights

Originally, weight training apparatus consisted of solid barbells (used with both hands) and dumb-bells (used with one hand). The weights often consisted of solid balls on the end of iron bars, and were used by strong men in circus acts at the turn of the century.

As training became more scientific, variable weights were needed; and so removable weight discs and collars were introduced.

Weight training bars

A barbell usually has three parts: the bar itself; weight discs; and small collars to secure the weights to the bar.

Standard exercise barbells are either adjustable, weights being added to change the total poundage of the bar, or fixed, with weights welded or bolted onto the bar. If the weight is fixed, a separate bar-bell is used for each five- or ten-pound weight increment.

For competitive weightlifting, or very heavy training, Olympic bars are used. These weigh 20 kg (45 lb), each collar being 2.5 kg (or 5.5 lb). Standard (non-Olympic) barbells are constructed around a steel bar about an inch thick and five or six feet long. These usually weigh between 25 and 30 lb.

The weight of the bar must be taken into account when calculating how much weight is lifted. For example, if you lifted a bar with a 10 lb weight on each end, you would be lifting not 20 lb, but as much as 50 lb allowing for the bar!

A tubular sleeve is often slipped over the bar to allow it to revolve freely without causing friction burns. Cross-hatched grooves or 'knurlings' may be cut into the sleeve, or directly onto the bar to provide a more secure grip.

Different-shaped bars are available to facilitate grip, and these are usually exercise specific. For arm curls and triceps extensions an 'EZ' bar may be used. This allows the hand to grip at an angle of 45° to the length of the bar, and both wide and narrow grips can be used. For pulley machines a wide-angled bar is available for the lateral pull-down, and a narrow-angled one for the triceps push-down. A narrow, square frame may be used for seated rowing.

Collars

Clamps or collars hold the weight discs in place. Inner collars are either welded to the bar or form part of the separate barbell sleeve. Outer collars hold the plates onto the bar, preventing them from sliding off during exercise.

Collars come in many shapes and sizes. Some have a threaded key, which is tightened to prevent the collar from slipping; others have a similar arrangement with the screw set flush with the collar and adjusted by an Allen key. The quick-release type are more convenient, however: these are 'spring clips', or keys which tighten in a single movement, and work in a similar way to the locking mechanism on the saddle-stem of a racing bicycle.

The bar itself can also be threaded, with the collar screwing directly onto it.

Dumb-bells are simply shorter versions of the barbell, intended for single-handed use. The bars are usually between 10 and 16 in long, and with collars weigh about 5 lb (again, remember to add this to the total weight lifted). A variety of plastic dumb-bells are available, including soft, rubberised versions for aerobic exercise.

Weight discs

There are various types of weight discs. Exercise discs are made of cast iron or steel, and have a hole 1 inch in diameter in the centre. They range in weight from 1.25 lb (0.5 kg) up to about 50 lb (20 or 25 kg). Olympic weight discs are similar in poundage, but have holes of 2 in to fit the larger Olympic bars.

Some discs are edged with rubber to protect the gymnasium floor, while others are made of solid rubber or special materials such as urethane. The solid-rubber Olympic discs are usually colour coded. Discs for home use may be of plastic-coated concrete; some are even bought as hollow plastic and filled with sand or water at home.

One of the advantages of free weights is their relatively low cost. They can be bought from most sports shops, and the advent of vinyl discs and plastic-coated bars means that a few pounds will now buy the beginner an adequate barbell and set of dumb-bells. Equipped with these, and some instructions on basic weight training exercises, a general programme can be started at home.

The main disadvantages here concern the safety of the user. Weights can be dropped and cause injury, and poor training techniques can cause sprains and pulls.

Multi-stack apparatus

The increasing interest in fitness over the last 30 years has led to the need for safer and more convenient forms of weight training. This has taken the shape of multi-stack weight training apparatus.

Weight stacks

In the case of free weights, discs are added or taken from a bar. With the multi-stack system, the poundage is changed by moving a selector key in a stack of weight blocks. These are usually marked in kilograms, but the weight shown does not necessarily take into account the leverage and friction forces involved, so may not reflect the true resistance being lifted.

Some manufacturers have started using 'split stacks', where the first three or four weights increase in units of 5 kg, and the rest in units of 10.

Many stacks now have guards in front of them to stop users, and particularly children, from trapping their fingers.

Pin selection

Instead of removable weight discs and collars, multi-stack apparatus uses a removable pin to alter the weight lifted. The pins sometimes have a locking device to stop them working loose. Some manufacturers attach the pin to a slide in front of the weight stack so that it cannot be removed from the machine; in some cases the pins are even magnetic.

Accommodating or variable resistance

In the case of free weights, the poundage exerted by the weight obviously stays the same throughout the whole movement. However, the force which a muscle can exert does not. This force will change as different leverage forces and muscle properties come into play during the movement.

Ideally, to build a muscle the resistance should be constant and at a maximum throughout the whole range of movement. This is not possible with a free weight, because the heaviest weight which can be lifted will be equal to the weakest point in the range of motion. For example, during an arm curl the leverage is maximal when the forearm is horizontal. At this point the weight will feel heaviest, and so this is the position which will govern the amount of weight which can be lifted. It constitutes the 'sticking point'.

At other points in the movement the leverage is less, and so the weight will feel lighter – at these points, then, more weight could be lifted. To make this possible the weight would have to change as it was being used, which obviously cannot happen when the weight is of a fixed amount. However, some multi-stack apparatus uses the principle of 'accommodating resistance' to alter the 'weight' as the movement occurs.

The aim of accommodating resistance is therefore to change the weight as the mechanical advantage of the muscle alters. To achieve this, certain exercise stations on multi-gyms have bars which travel through an arc as the weight is lifted. At the bottom position (the beginning of the movement) the lever arm is greatest. As the weight is pushed up, the lever arm reduces and so the resistance to be overcome is greater.

Cam-operated machines

Accommodating resistance ensures that the weight lifted is gradually increased in a fairly simple fashion. This feature is extended in the case of cam-operated machines. Here, the shape of the cam is designed to alter the resistance so that it mimics the changes in strength of a particular muscle.

This has advantages in that the overload can be nearer to maximum throughout the range of motion. However, it also means that a separate machine is usually needed for each muscle group. This reduces the variety of exercises available, and increases the expense of providing adequate apparatus.

Hydraulics and pneumatics

Another way of providing resistance is to use hydraulic (fluid) or pneumatic (air) pressure.

With hydraulics, fluid is forced from one chamber into another. The higher the speed of movement, the greater the resistance imposed, so that this type of apparatus does offer the advantage of accommodating resistance. The leverage is changed by moving the distance of attachment of the hydraulic cylinder further away from or closer to the pivot of the machine. Unfortunately, no eccentric component is possible during this type of training: after a bar is pushed up, the opposite (antagonist) muscle group is used to pull the bar down again.

With pneumatics, the resistance is supplied by compressed air created by an electric pump. Resistance is variable, and both concentric and eccentric work is involved.

Both of these types of machine are fairly silent in use; this is seen by some as a disadvantage, because it affects the 'atmosphere' in the gym and reduces the motivation of users. Others see silent operation as a benefit, and claim that the apparatus is safer to use than traditional free-weight or multi-stack apparatus.

CHAPTER 9

Weight training practice

Before exercising, it is important to look at some basic weight training practices and to become familiar with the general terms that will form our 'weight training vocabulary'.

Sets and reps

Each time a weight is lifted a repetition or 'rep' is performed. A number of reps grouped together is called a 'set'. Each set is usually followed by a recovery period.

Traditionally, low numbers of repetitions (4–10) are used to increase strength, while higher numbers (15–25) are used to improve muscle endurance.

There are no magical combinations of sets and reps which will instantly give the desired results. It is very much up to each individual to find the ideal combination for him. This comes with experience, and you must be prepared to change rep/set combinations as you develop. As a general guide for beginners training to improve strength or muscle tone, the weight should be increased when you are able to lift it more than 12–15 times. For best results when strength training, a muscle must be overloaded by working it to fatigue. When you first start training, a specific number of reps may be enough; as you get more experienced, and more able to increase the intensity of your training, you should only stop training when no more can be lifted.

Frequency, intensity and duration

During resistance training slight damage occurs within the muscle itself. In order to repair itself the muscle needs time, so training should be performed on a particular muscle group every other day. Three sessions per week of resistance training is generally sufficient for maximal strength gains.

During the rest period between each set, fresh blood is flushed into the muscle to remove metabolic wastes and to replenish the muscle's energy stores.

When working sub-maximally, a recovery of between 30 and 60 seconds is generally sufficient between sets, but this period will obviously increase when maximal work is performed or as fatigue sets in. At the beginning of a work-out you are still fresh, so less rest is needed; by the end, however, rest periods should be increased as you tire. It takes about 3 minutes to 'pay back' most of a muscle's local energy stores, so the muscle will not be fully recovered until this time period has elapsed.

Weight training is a predominantly anaerobic activity and therefore it quickly uses up the body's energy stores. The duration of this type of training should usually be between 30 minutes and 1 hour. Longer periods tend to be of lower quality and of little further benefit.

Timing

When trying to strengthen or tone a muscle using weight training apparatus we must capitalise on all three types of muscle work – *concentric, isometric* and *eccentric*. Concentric work occurs when a weight is lifted; isometric as it is held; and eccentric as the weight is lowered under control (*see* pp. 35–36).

If the exercise is performed too quickly the eccentric phase may be too short and the isometric phase missed out altogether. This sometimes happens when the weight is lifted and then almost 'dropped' by an inexperienced user.

The best way to ensure that all three types of work are done is to lift for a count of two, to hold for one, and to lower for a count of four. In the case of some advanced training techniques the lowering period is extended to increase the intensity of work done by the muscle.

Order of exercises

In a basic routine, large muscle groups should be exercised first. The small muscles will be the first to fatigue: because they form the final link in the chain of movement, exercise will stop before the large groups reach exhaustion.

For example, both the pectorals and the triceps are exercised during a bench press. However, were you to perform a triceps isolation exercise before the bench press, the triceps would fatigue, thus limiting the number of reps possible on the bench press and therefore the work done by the biceps.

In any work-out, the 'priority' muscles – those with which you are particularly concerned – should be worked first. If your primary aim is to build up leg strength, and your secondary aim is to maintain general body tone, then leg exercises should be performed first.

For general fitness training the heart rate should be kept high, but muscles should still be allowed to recover after they have been worked. This is achieved by working the different body areas in turn (arms, legs, trunk, then repeat). In this way, individual muscles recover but overall body activity keeps the heart rate high and thus improves stamina.

Type of exercise

Exercises can be classified broadly as being one of two types: *basic* (multi-joint) exercises and *isolation* (single-joint) exercises.

Basic exercises move a number of joints, and so exercise a whole range of muscles. Examples include the bench press, the squat, and the shoulder press. Isolation exercises focus on one muscle by trying to restrict the movement to one joint. Examples include dumb-bell flyes, leg extensions and lateral raises. Various basic and isolation exercises are presented in table 5.

Table 5   Types of exercise

Basic exercise	Isolation exercise
Squat	Leg extension
Leg press	Leg curl
Lunge	Hip abduction
Bench press	Vertical flye
Shoulder press	Dumb-bell lateral raise
Dips	Triceps extension
Chin-ups	Arm curl

Speed of movement

In any resistance training programme the aim is to overload a muscle by getting it to lift a weight. Fast, jerky actions will increase the weight's momentum. This additional force can then be used to help lift the weight, so that less work is done by the muscle, and ultimately less benefit gained from the training.

Furthermore, as momentum builds up it becomes more difficult to stop a movement. When fatigue sets in, the increased momentum working at the end of the movement range can over-stretch and tear at the joint structures, causing injury.

Breathing

The general rule is **breathe out on effort**. As a weight is lifted the muscle bulges, increasing the resistance to blood flow and so raising the blood pressure. If at this stage you hold your breath, your blood pressure will increase still further. If you breathe out, the resultant reduction in abdominal pressure will limit this increase.

Although this is a general rule for safety, there are two occasions on which it will not apply. The first is when you are working for chest expansion, for example with a pull-over or a dumb-bell flye. When performing these exercises you should breathe in.

The second instance concerns the valsalva manoeuvre. This is a specialised weight-lifting technique, during which the athlete holds his breath and then tries to breathe out against a closed glottis. The increased intra-thoracic pressure and raised blood pressure give a feeling of strength, and may lessen the likelihood of injury to the spinal discs. However, this may cause light-headedness and therefore should be avoided by all but the most experienced users.

CHAPTER 10

Weight training programmes

Basic training programmes

When compiling any weight training programme it is important to have a clear idea of what you are trying to achieve. A programme designed to improve general fitness and muscle tone will differ from one designed to increase strength. Some individuals may be training to improve their performance at a particular sport, whilst others may want to lose weight. Training must therefore be adapted accordingly.

Progressive resistance training

The traditional concept of 'progressive resistance exercise' was first developed after the Second World War by two doctors, Delorme and Watkins. Although intended at the time to be used in rehabilitation, the techniques have since become the standard for all types of muscle training.

The method first requires the user to discover the maximum weight which can be lifted ten times – the *10 rep max* (10RM). This is established for each exercise by trial and error (*see* 'Gym Tests', pp. 134–137). The training programme then consists of 3 sets of 10 repetitions at percentages of this maximal value, as follows:

- 1st set: 10 reps at 50% of 10RM;
- 2nd set: 10 reps at 75% of 10RM;
- 3rd set: 10 reps at 100% of 10RM.

After each set you should rest and allow your breathing rate to return to normal. Early in the training programme this will happen fairly quickly, but as you work through your routine the amount of rest you need after each set will increase.

Although the calculation required by this type of training can be time-consuming, it does give the novice user some guidance as to how to progress. It does not take long to get used to the percentages used, and to be able to 'feel' the difference in poundage between the three sets.

The programme ensures that you are fully warmed up before you attempt your 100% maximum lift, and so lessens the likelihood of injury.

Pyramid training

In the case of pyramid training, the amount of weight which can be lifted just once (1 rep max or 1RM) is calculated. A percentage of this value is then lifted for each set. The number of repetitions performed in each set is reduced as the weight increases (in contrast to 'Descending Sets', see page 78), as follows:

- 1st set: 12 reps at 50% 1RM;
- 2nd set: 8 reps at 65% 1RM;
- 3rd set: 6 reps at 75% 1RM, or to fatigue.

The weight is still increased, as it is with the Delorme and Watkins regime; this time, however, the number of reps is reduced so that the amount of weight which can be lifted – and therefore the muscle overload – is greater. Enough rest should be taken after each set to allow the breathing rate to return to normal.

Circuit training

The two programmes described above were designed simply to increase strength and muscle tone. If the training aim is to tone up and keep fit, circuit training should be performed.

Circuit training consists of a number of exercises performed in a continuous sequence, with very little rest between each. This type of training emphasises the stamina component of fitness training by keeping the heart rate high and so increasing the amount of aerobic activity.

The circuit can be seen as a structured form of group exercise; a sort of 'regulated aerobics class' that can easily be controlled by an instructor and can be performed in a confined space. Instead of resting after each set, allowing the muscle to recover and letting the heart rate fall, the aim of circuit training is to increase the heart rate and to keep it high. This is achieved by working the various parts of the body in sequence (arms/legs/trunk) without any rest period which allows the heart rate to drop significantly.

Designing general fitness circuits

A variety of free exercises or apparatus may be used, incorporating different fitness components. Exercises for strength may be interspersed with flexibility, stamina, speed and skill work to give an overall work-out. Simple exercises such as push-ups and sit-ups become more challenging in a circuit format, and specificity of training may be enhanced by mimicking the actions involved in a particular sport. For example, a circuit may be set up on a football pitch involving short sprints, zig-zag running, dribbling, and shooting skills, in addition to upper body and trunk work.

The circuit may be developed by altering the frequency (number of complete circuits), intensity (resistance, heart rate, range of motion) or duration (number of repetitions) of the various exercises. Either set the number of repetitions, in which case the aim is to complete the circuit as quickly as possible; or specify a time limit with the aim of performing the greatest possible number of repetitions.

Organising the circuit

One method of organising the circuit is for each individual to perform a fitness test on the exercises which will comprise the circuit. The individual works to his or her maximum capacity, and the score obtained determines the number of repetitions to be performed during training. In this manner, individuals of various fitness levels are able to train together, each performing the same exercises but at different intensities. In addition, the scores obtained for each exercise may form part of a general fitness evaluation which can be repeated at regular intervals to assess progress. This can be particularly useful in team sports if the first test is performed at the beginning of a season and the repeat evaluations used as a factor in team selection.

The circuit may be set out by sketching each exercise in performance using 'pin-men' figures, and then writing a brief explanation of each movement beneath. This information is then placed at the relevant exercise station. Large clear figures should be used, and it can be useful to use colour coding for easy recognition, dividing up the circuit participants into beginners (blue), intermediate (green) and advanced (red). At each station the exercise type or number of repetitions can be represented by a colour, as follows.

- Same exercise, but varying number of repetitions.
  BLUE: 10 reps
  GREEN: 12 reps
  RED: 15 reps

- Same number of reps, but different starting positions.
  BLUE: Push-up from kneeling
  GREEN: Standard push-up
  RED: Push-up with feet on stool

Circuit weight training

Instead of using all types of exercise, circuit weight training (CWT) is performed using only resistance training apparatus. In contrast to normal weight training, CWT places less emphasis on heavy over-load of a single muscle group, using instead a more general fitness programme. Work on arms, legs and trunk is alternated to prevent fatigue in any one muscle group, but constant activity is maintained so that the heart rate stays high. Various types of work:rest ratio may be used. Typical combinations would be eight or more exercises, with a weight of 40–55% 1RM. As many repetitions as possible should be performed in 30 seconds, for example, with a rest of 15 seconds.

Only small increases in cardio-pulmonary fitness should be expected with this type of training, but CWT has been shown to be particularly effective in helping to maintain fitness and so has an important part to play in rehabilitation. Because of the controlled nature of the activity, it is possible to focus on or to exclude specific parts of the body while still working the rest. This is particularly useful during injury, as general physical condition can be maintained without placing stress on the injured part. For example, if a person has a hamstring injury, specific physiotherapy would be used for the leg, and CWT performed to maintain fitness in the upper body and trunk. Later, a full circuit may be initiated to develop competitive fitness of the whole body.

Advanced training techniques

If you are training for strength, and have been using weights for some time, you will need to integrate some advanced training techniques into your programme. This is because muscles must be regularly challenged if they are to continue to gain in strength. Eventually, the basic programmes become too easy. Advanced strength training techniques aim to make your muscles work harder, and can be seen as the 'icing on the cake' of your training programme. Try some of the following techniques, and use them to introduce variety into your schedule.

Working past fatigue

Forced repetitions: Use a training partner to assist you past the 'sticking point' in an exercise. When you get to the point at which you are no longer able to move a weight, your partner can help by just taking the weight slightly on the upwards movement. This should be a slight touch of the bar, in effect momentarily reducing the weight you have to lift.

Negative work: The eccentric or negative action of a muscle is the most powerful, and is the last to be fatigued. The force produced is greater than that of either concentric or isometric action, and so should be the most efficient at building strength. In addition, eccentric work forms the basis for plyometric training (see pp. 81–82).

Research has shown that working eccentrically, and therefore lifting more weight than you would be able to during normal training, can give you greater strength gains. However, there is a cost. Muscle soreness results from this type of training, and the use of heavier weights makes you more prone to injury – so take care! It is better to combine all types of muscle work – eccentric, concentric and isometric – during a training session.

To perform negative work during your general exercise programme, lift a weight normally until you feel fatigued and then get a training partner to help you hold it as you lower it under control. Negative reps can also be carried out without assistance for exercises such as dips and chin-ups. With these exercises you simply lift yourself up using your legs and then lower yourself with your arms only.

'Cheating' reps: Strict exercise form should usually be encouraged to minimise the risk of injury. Sometimes, however, other muscles can be used to assist the lifter in overcoming the sticking point and continuing to fatigue. This is only appropriate if the movement produced is safely different from the standard form.

For example, if you are performing a biceps curl, and the sticking point occurs as your forearm reaches the horizontal, you can get past this point by rapidly bending and then straightening your legs and using momentum to help lift the weight. This is useful at the end of a set, but if the small movement becomes a large, swinging action of the spine this can be dangerous. Seek assistance from a training partner, or stop.

Descending sets: Instead of using a constant weight, reduce the weight as fatigue sets in. This technique is particularly useful when training with multi-stack apparatus, because the weight is easily adjusted by moving the selector pin.

For example, while performing a shoulder press facing the weight stack, do 5 reps at 35 kg, 3 at 30 kg, 2 at 25 kg and the last at only 20 kg. Each change in weight should be made as rapidly as possible so the muscle does not have a chance to rest.

This technique is more difficult when using free weights, because two training partners are needed to take weights off quickly – one at each end of the bar.

Changing the order of exercises

Supersets: With this type of training, blood is kept within a particular area of the body by working opposing muscle groups alternatively. For example, the triceps are worked for one set, then the biceps are worked immediately afterwards. This pattern continues for three sets.

Split routines: Only certain parts of the body are worked in each session. This means that you are able to train daily, or even twice a day in some cases. For example, you may chose to work on the arms, chest and shoulders on one day, and the legs, back and trunk the next.

Split routines can last from three to six days, but at least one day a week should be set aside for rest. Examples of split routines used in bodybuilding are shown in table 6.

Pre-exhaust training

When you perform a basic exercise for the large torso muscles such as the chest, shoulders, or hips, you are also working smaller limb

Table 6   Examples of split routines

Alternative 1	
Monday–Thursday	*Tuesday–Friday*
Abdominals (hard)	Abdominals (easy)
Chest	Thighs
Shoulders	Arms
Back	Calves

Alternative 2	
Monday–Thursday	*Tuesday–Friday*
Calves	Abdominals
Chest	Thighs
Shoulders	Back
Triceps	Biceps
Forearms	

Alternative 3	
Monday–Thursday	*Tuesday–Friday*
Abdominals (hard)	Calves
Thighs	Back
Chest	Shoulders
Biceps	Triceps
Forearms	Abdominals (easy)

muscles like those of the arms and thighs. Unfortunately, the smaller muscles will fatigue before the larger ones have been worked maximally.

To compensate for this it is possible partially to exhaust the large muscles by performing an isolation movement before continuing to train them to fatigue with the basic movement. This is known as *pre-exhaust* training.

Take as an example the deltoids of the shoulder. To work these, you would start by performing lateral raises to fatigue; you would then progress immediately (without a recovery period) to shoulder pressing. In the first instance the deltoids are working almost in isolation; in the second, they work with the triceps.

Periodisation

Training in the same way all the time can lead to boredom and stagnation, with physical development reaching a plateau. With periodisation it is possible to concentrate on certain types of training at particular times in the year, allowing one stage of training to progress into another.

Four categories are generally used.

● Pre-season training.
● Early season training.
● Peak season training.
● Off-season training.

The aim is to cover all the components of fitness, and to build to a peak just before competition.

The first phase is the preparatory phase, divided into *pre-season* and *early season* training. Pre-season training lasts for about four months; early season training for about one month. As an athlete approaches his/her peak season, more skill training and sport-specific work is included.

During the peak or competitive season, training will be designed to maintain the particular fitness and skill needed for competition.

Off-season training acts as a recovery period, psychologically refreshing the athlete and allowing the body to slow down after the intense demands of competition. The timing of this period will depend on the type of sport. During off-season training moderate activity should be maintained so that the progress made in the other periods is not lost.

Although this type of training was designed originally for competitive athletes, benefits can still be obtained by fitness enthusiasts. For example, the casual tennis player can concentrate on weight training in his pre-season training, in order to build up a foundation of strength. Fitness training can be brought in during early training, and skill training introduced. Skill training comes to the fore during the peak season, while strength training is usually dropped.

Tennis should not be played during the off-season period so that the player has a psychological break. Instead, light weight training begins again in preparation for the heavy strength training of the pre-season cycle.

Training for power and speed

Most weight training is performed in a slow, controlled fashion, and this increases strength, or 'the ability to overcome an external resistance'. However, in sport there is an additional factor to be considered – the speed at which a movement is carried out. When a fast action occurs against a resistance (in this case the weight) we are training for power. Working for power involves using a rapid explosive action. Obviously a lighter weight is used, and considerable attention must be paid to safety factors.

Eccentric actions may be combined with power training. The muscle is first stretched, in order to 'load' it, and then it is contracted rapidly. This type of action occurs in many sports. For example, when throwing, an athlete will reach the arm behind the body to 'wind up' for the throw. As the arm comes forwards it moves rapidly until the ball or other implement is released. Speed training which involves pre-loading the muscle before rapid contraction is known as *plyometrics*.

Plyometrics

Plyometrics was first popularised by the eastern bloc countries for the development of speed in athletes. It consists of a rapid eccentric contraction performed immediately before an explosive concentric action, for example lowering quickly into a squatting position and then immediately jumping back to standing. This type of movement involves pre-stretching a muscle, affecting both its contractile and inert structures.

The rapid stretch stimulates a protective reflex mechanism in the muscle, which in turn generates greater tension as the muscle contracts. As the muscle is slightly elastic, the release of the 'muscle spring' makes the concentric contraction greater than it would be in isolation. The use of muscle contraction involving acceleration in the concentric phase and deceleration in the eccentric phase mirrors the sporting action more closely, and therefore has advantages in terms of training specificity.

Practical considerations of plyometric training

Plyometric exercise is only effective when the concentric contraction occurs immediately following the pre-stretch cycle. If the movement is not continuous, some of the training benefits will be lost as elastic energy is wasted and the effect of the stretch reflex altered. This type of training is intense, and should only be used after a thorough warm-up. To perform plyometrics the athlete needs a good strength base, and his balancing abilities should be tested before training commences. If he lacks a good sense of balance he may fall as fatigue sets in. Other safety considerations include proper clothing and footwear, and a flat, firm, non-slip surface.

Three types of exercises are normally used: *in-place*, *short-response*, and *long-response*. In-place activities include such things as standing jumps, drop jumps and hopping; the athlete performs the activity largely 'on the spot' and may adapt them for weight training. Short-response actions are those which cover some distance, such as standing long jump, standing triple jump and box jumps. Long-response movements cover a greater distance and include bounding, hopping and repeated hurdle jumps.

Although plyometric activity is primarily used for lower limb training, it does have an important place in the development of the upper limbs and trunk. Overhead throwing actions using a medicine ball, and throwing and catching from a bent-knee sit-up position are good examples.

Resistance may be added to increase the overload of the working muscles during plyometric activity. Vertical jumps may be performed using light dumb-bells or a squat/leg press machine, and horizontal movements (lateral jumps, side hops) can be overloaded using an elastic cord. Obviously momentum is considerably greater when using weights at speed, and safety must be emphasised.

A good example of plyometric training with added resistance is as follows: a light squat is performed with a dumb-bell held in either hand. The athlete lowers into the half-squat position fairly quickly, keeping the movement controlled. He then jumps as high as possible, reducing his speed of movement as he lowers again. In the case of the leg press, the weight is lowered until the knees contact the chest, and then the legs straighten rapidly (be careful not to hyperextend). The foot may lose contact with the leg-press plate, so when the weight is 'caught' again the knees should be slightly flexed. This gives some spring and avoids jarring the knees and hips.

PART TWO

Practical Application

CHAPTER 11

The exercises

This section describes the various exercises which can be used in training. The list is by no means exhaustive, but deals with the most commonly encountered movements. Each is described in terms of major muscles used, additional muscles used, starting position, technique, variations, and points to note.

Muscles used

This refers to the training effect of the exercise only. Other muscles will be involved in the movement as part of the group action, but their involvement is not generally important for standard training.

Before each section, a brief review of the structure and function of the region is included. However, it is always of use to go to an anatomy book to improve your knowledge of the muscles you are using.

Starting position

Before starting an exercise it is important to set up the equipment correctly for both safety and comfort. Make sure that the machine is adjusted to suit you so that there is no need to stop and change things once you have started to exercise.

Safety measures include taking up a position which is stable. When standing, your feet should be apart and facing in the direction of the movement. For example, when a dumb-bell lateral raise is performed, your feet should be astride (it is a sideways movement). With a single-arm pulley row, your feet can be one in front of the other as the movement is forwards and back. In either case your feet should be apart and flat on the floor to give a good base of support.

Do a basic equipment check before you lift the weight. Check that weight collars are tight, selector pins are secure, and adjustment levers are locked. Finally, make sure that nobody is near enough to you to be hit with the weight you are lifting.

Technique

This book has stressed the importance of lifting, holding, and slowly lowering a weight to get the most benefit from each repetition. As well as being a more effective form of training, this reduces momentum and therefore lessens the risk of injury.

When you have been training for a while, you will need to try some of the advanced techniques described in Chapter 10, such as forced and descending reps.

To begin with, many of the free exercises are more usefully performed in front of a mirror so that you can check your posture and exercise technique. Take care that you do not stand so close that you hit the mirror when using a large range of motion!

Variations

Variations of exercises are included because these prevent you from getting stale. You will prefer certain exercises; some will suit you more than others. This is fine, and serves to individualise your weight training programme.

Points to note

This section explains any idiosyncrasies possessed by a particular exercise, and is particularly important because these often raise the questions of safety and injury prevention. You may like to make a note of any points you find relevant to your own training style after reading this section.

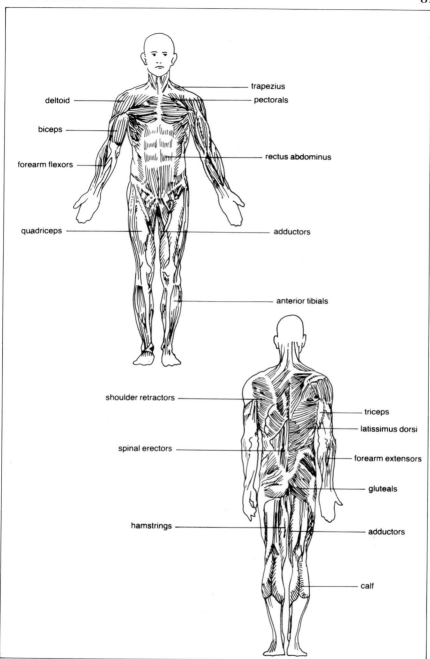

Fig. 26 Major muscles of the body

CHAPTER 12

The upper limb

The upper limb consists of the shoulder blade and collar bone, the upper arm, the forearm, and the wrist and hand. The whole limb is designed to facilitate grip. All the complex movements of the shoulder and arm occur so that the hand can be positioned easily and precisely. When the hand is in position the complex structure of the fingers and thumb allows us to grip powerfully and with great precision. It is this feature more than any other which separates man from other animals.

To enable the arm to be raised over the head, the shoulder joint will allow the upper arm bone to swing out to the horizontal position. After this, the shoulder blade itself starts to slide over the back of the rib-cage, moving the arm above the head. When the shoulder is injured it is often this mechanism which loses its power, and the arm becomes painful as it approaches head height.

The shoulder is a ball-and-socket joint and as such is very mobile. It is also very strong. To allow both functions to co-exist, a set of muscles called the *rotator cuff* lies close to the joint and acts as 'active ligaments' to help hold the joint together.

The large *deltoid* muscle pulls the arm away from the side of the body. Consisting of front, side and back parts, it surrounds the shoulder; it is important to exercise all parts of this muscle. The *latissimus* muscle lying under the arm and down the side of the body pulls the arm back into the side, and is worked in exercises such as chin-ups and lateral pull-downs.

   The *trapezius* lies between the shoulder and neck, and will shrug
the shoulder and help to pull it back. Muscles between the shoulder
blades brace the shoulders, and are important for good posture.

   The massive *pectorals* are the pushing and punching muscles.
They have two parts attaching to the collar and breast bones, both
of which can be exercised in all types of bench press.

   The arm bends and straightens mainly as a result of the action of
the biceps and triceps, but both of these muscles can also help to
move the shoulder.

   The forearm can twist; as it does so, the forearm bones cross over
each other. The muscles of the forearm will move the wrist and
hand. Those on the front of the forearm will bend the fingers and
facilitate grip, and those on the back straighten the fingers. The
muscles of the forearm and the hand are used to a varying extent
in most weight training exercises.

The bench press

MAJOR MUSCLE GROUPS WORKED: Pectorals
ADDITIONAL MUSCLES USED: Triceps; anterior/medial deltoids
STARTING POSITION: Lie on a flat bench with a barbell or the bar of a Universal machine level with your upper chest. Take an 'over-grasp' grip. Your knees should be bent and your feet flat on the floor.
TECHNIQUE: Bend your arms, allowing your elbows to travel out to the sides. Lower the bar down and slightly forwards, to upper-chest level. Do not bounce the weight. Pause, and then slowly press the weight up, straightening the arms.
BREATHING: Breathe in as the weight is lowered onto your chest; breathe out as you push it up.
VARIATIONS: A wider grip will increase the emphasis on the pectoral muscles; a narrower grip places more stress on the triceps.

Inclined bench presses (shoulders above hips), performed on a bench angled at between 15 and 60°, will increase the work done by the upper pectorals (*clavicular* fibres) and anterior deltoids.

Declined bench presses (shoulders lower than hips) place greater emphasis on the lower and outer part of the pectorals (*sternal* fibres).

Points to note: Try to avoid raising the small of your back from the bench. This can compress the joints of the lower spine and cause problems later.

To avoid lifting your back off the bench, modify your starting position by bending your knees and placing your feet flat on the bench, or by pulling your legs up so that your hips are at 90° to your body.

Bench press

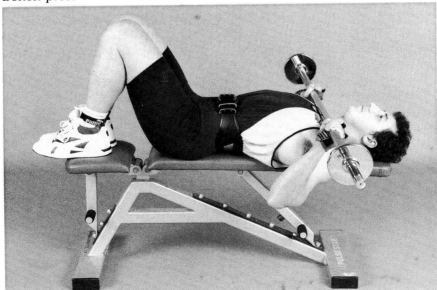

Seated bench press

Inclined bench press

The 'pec deck' (vertical flye)

MAJOR MUSCLE GROUPS WORKED: Pectorals

ADDITIONAL MUSCLES USED: Anterior deltoids

STARTING POSITION: Adjust the seat height of the machine so that your feet are flat on the floor or supported on the foot pedal. Your elbows should be bent to about 90°, with your upper arms parallel to the floor and your hands gripping the outside/upper edge of the machine arm-pad. Your back should be flat against the back-pad of the machine.

TECHNIQUE: Press with the whole of your forearm to bring the pads together in front of your chest. Hold this contracted position momentarily, and then slowly release the pads to stretch the pecs once more.

BREATHING: Breathe out as you bring the pads together, and in as they return and your chest is expanded.

VARIATIONS: Altering the seat height and therefore the angle of your arm will vary the muscular emphasis of the exercise. Performing the same movement single-handed will increase the intensity of the movement. Sitting the other way around on the stool and pushing backwards with the backs of the arms will exercise the posterior scapular muscles.

The 'pec deck' (vertical flye)

Points to note: On some machines the initial stretch is too great for less flexible individuals. In this case the pads should be drawn together slightly without the selector pin in the machine. If the pin is then positioned so that a gap is left between the weight blocks, the pulley wire will slacken slightly. However, be cautious that the wire does not come off the pulleys of the machine.

Dumb-bell flyes

MAJOR MUSCLE GROUPS WORKED: Pectorals
ADDITIONAL MUSCLES USED: Anterior deltoids
STARTING POSITION: Lie on a flat bench with your knees shoulder-width apart and your feet flat on the floor. Grip a light dumb-bell in each hand above your upper chest. Keep your arms slightly bent (elbows 'unlocked'), with the palms of your hands facing each other.
TECHNIQUE: Slowly lower the dumb-bells out sideways, letting them descend in an arc to the same level as your head. Without bouncing when the lowest position is reached, slowly raise the weights back to the starting point.
BREATHING: Breathe in as you lower the weights and expand your chest; breathe out as your arms come together again.

Dumb-bell flyes. When a heavy weight is used, a training partner should kneel at the head end of the bench and cup the athlete's elbows in his or her hands. Support can then be given at the point of maximum stretch as the arms are fully lowered

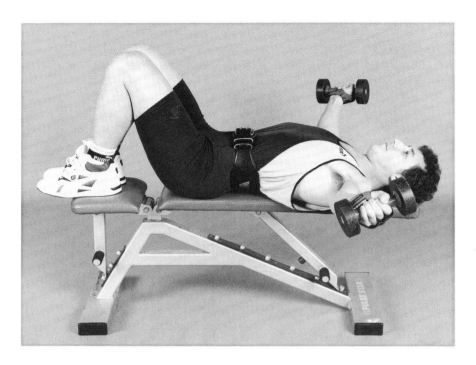

VARIATIONS: As with the bench press, this exercise can be performed inclined or declined. Inclined dumb-bell flyes will place greater emphasis on the upper pectorals, while declined dumb-bell flyes will work the lower pectorals.

Points to note: Because of the leverage involved in this exercise, light weights only should be used to begin with. To make the exercise easier with the same weight, bend the elbow further, shortening the leverage effect on your arm. See the bench press (page 90) for points to note concerning the spine.

The shoulder press

MAJOR MUSCLE GROUPS WORKED: Deltoids, triceps
ADDITIONAL MUSCLES USED: Upper pectorals, muscles surrounding scapulae
STARTING POSITION: Begin with a barbell or multi-gym shoulder bar resting on or just above your shoulders. Your hands should be slightly wider than shoulder-width apart. Keep your elbows directly beneath your upper arms, and use a 'thumb-under' or 'thumb-round' grip. The exercise can be performed standing, but is more commonly performed sitting.

TECHNIQUE: Press the bar directly upwards, taking it just in front of your face. Lock the arms out overhead and then bring the bar down slowly.

BREATHING: Breathe out as you press the bar overhead, and in as the bar descends.

VARIATIONS: You can change the effect of the exercise slightly by altering your grip, and by performing the movement with a free weight, Universal machine, Smith machine or with dumb-bells held in each hand.

From the same starting position, the bar can be lowered behind the neck to shoulder level. This exercise increases the emphasis on the posterior deltoids and scapular muscles.

Points to note: There is always a tendency to over-arch the spine with this exercise. This is best avoided by adhering to good technique, and by not being tempted to increase the weight too soon. In addition, a weight training belt should be worn, and the abdominal muscles held tight throughout the movement.

Some individuals may find that their shoulders click as they perform this exercise. This is usually due either to the formation of gas bubbles in the joint fluid of the shoulder, or to a tendon flicking over a bony knobble a little bit like a guitar string. Both situations are harmless provided that they do not cause pain. If pain does occur, the shoulder structures may become inflamed; so rest or miss this exercise out of your programme until you can perform it in comfort.

Upright row

MAJOR MUSCLE GROUPS WORKED: Deltoids (medial head), trapezius

ADDITIONAL MUSCLES USED: Biceps, scapular muscles, forearm flexors

STARTING POSITION: Hold a barbell or the exercise bar of a lower pulley unit with your hands about 15–20 cm apart. Stand erect, with your feet shoulder-width apart.

TECHNIQUE: Pull the bar upwards, moving it close to your body until the backs of your hands almost touch your chin. Keep your elbows above your wrists throughout the movement. Pause briefly at the top of the movement before lowering the weight in a controlled fashion.

BREATHING: Breathe out as you lift, and in as you lower the weight.

Upright row

VARIATIONS: A wider grip will place greater emphasis on the deltoids and less on the trapezius. With a wide (0.5 m) grip you should raise the bar to upper-chest level only.

Points to note: Using a lighter weight, you can reverse your breathing pattern (in as you lift, out as you lower) and concentrate on chest expansion.

Lateral raises

MAJOR MUSCLE GROUPS WORKED: Medial head of deltoids
ADDITIONAL MUSCLES USED: Anterior deltoid, trapezius
STARTING POSITION: Hold a light dumb-bell in each hand, with the end of the dumb-bell facing forwards and your hands in front of your thighs. Stand with your feet shoulder-width apart.
TECHNIQUE: Slowly raise the dumb-bells out to the sides in a semicircular motion. Keep your elbows slightly bent (10–15°) if you feel any strain on them. Continue the lift until your hands reach shoulder level; at this stage allow the front plate of the dumb-bell to dip down slightly to cause a medial rotation of the shoulder joint. Pause in this position, then slowly lower the weights.
BREATHING: Breathe out as the dumb-bells are lifted, and in as they are lowered.

VARIATIONS: Use lighter weights and take the dumb-bells overhead: breathe in as the weight is lifted to expand your chest.

Lateral raises can be performed single-handed, with the free hand holding onto a machine-upright to eliminate upper-body sway. The single-handed movement can also be performed holding the loop handle of a low pulley machine (*cable lateral raise*).

Points to note: Maintain strict form with this exercise. Swinging the weights or using weights which are too heavy will build up a lot of momentum. This can be dangerous and may cause inflammation in the shoulder tendons. The same points made with the shoulder press concerning joint clicking apply to this exercise (*see* page 95).

Lateral raise. This subject is using a light weight and has chosen to lock his elbows. Normally the elbows should be slightly bent to reduce the stress placed on the joints

Pull-overs

MAJOR MUSCLE GROUPS WORKED: Latissimus dorsi, pectorals
ADDITIONAL MUSCLES USED: Scapular muscles
STARTING POSITION: Hold a dumb-bell between both hands and lie across a flat bench with just your shoulders supported. Place your knees wide apart with your feet flat on the floor, and ensure that your hips are below bench level.
TECHNIQUE: Keeping the elbows slightly bent, lower the dumb-bell overhead towards the floor. Without bouncing, pause in the lower position and then pull the weight back to the starting position.
BREATHING: Breathe in as you pull the dumb-bell overhead; breathe out as you return it to the starting position.
VARIATIONS: This exercise can be performed lying flat on the floor and holding a barbell or two dumb-bells. This variation exerts less pressure on the chest muscles.

Some manufacturers produce pull-over machines which have a similar effect, but which have pads for the elbows to push down on.
Points to note: Start with a very light weight until you are confident about your chest flexibility. Older individuals who are new to weight training should avoid heavy weights if they have a particularly tight ribcage.

Pull-overs. Where a heavy weight is used, a training partner should be positioned at the athlete's head to support the weight as it approaches the fully stretched position near the floor

The pull-over machine

Seated rowing

MAJOR MUSCLE GROUPS WORKED: Latissimus dorsi, trapezius, posterior deltoids

ADDITIONAL MUSCLES USED: Biceps, scapular muscles, forearms

STARTING POSITION: Sit on the floor facing a low pulley unit. Keep your knees bent and your back straight. Grip a straight exercise bar or a close-grip rowing handle.

TECHNIQUE: Pull the bar towards you, at the same time sitting up straight and tensing your back muscles. Keep your elbows close in to your sides. Pause, then allow the weight to lower, straightening your arms and allowing your back and shoulders to 'round' again.

BREATHING: Breathe in as you pull (expanding the chest), and out as you release.

VARIATIONS: A wider bar can be used, with the elbows held level with the shoulders. This reduces the emphasis on the latissimus dorsi and increases the work done by the posterior deltoids and trapezius.

Points to note: The knees should be kept bent so that the lower spine remains hollow throughout the movement. If the legs are straightened, tightness in the hamstrings will tip the pelvis backwards and round the lower back.

This exercise is excellent for correcting faulty posture from rounded shoulders.

Seated rowing machine

Lateral pull-downs

MAJOR MUSCLE GROUPS WORKED: Latissimus dorsi
ADDITIONAL MUSCLES USED: Biceps, rear shoulder muscles, forearms
STARTING POSITION: Various types of bar can be used, to facilitate wide or narrow grips and more or less movement. The most usual is the straight bar which is angled down about 15 cm from each end.

Take hold of the angled parts of the bar with your hands comfortably wider than shoulder-width apart. Either kneel down on the floor or sit on a bench, and start with the arms straight. Some machines will have rollers to hold the knees down.

TECHNIQUE: Pull the bar down smoothly, with minimal trunk movement, until it rests across the shoulders. Pause, and then slowly allow the bar to move up again, maintaining tension in the muscles.

BREATHING: Breathe out as you pull the bar towards you, and in as the weight is lowered.

VARIATIONS: The bar can be taken level to the upper chest (*front pull-down*). A narrow-grip bar can be used, the handles of which are parallel and about 10 cm long (*close-grip pull-down*).

The front pull-down places greater emphasis on the anterior deltoids; while the close-grip pull-down tends to thicken the latissimus dorsi rather than widening them.

Points to note: It is important to tie hair well back and remove neck chains before performing this exercise, as these may catch on the wire or bar with tragic results.

These exercises build the upper back and posterior shoulder muscles, and are particularly useful in correcting postural problems such as round shoulders. They are also used in rehabilitation after some types of back injury.

Lateral pull-down

Chin-ups

MAJOR MUSCLE GROUPS WORKED: Latissimus   dorsi,   biceps   and brachialis
ADDITIONAL MUSCLES USED: Posterior deltoids, forearms
STARTING POSITION: Start by grippping a chinning bar, hands shoulder-width apart and arms straight. Bend the knees to 90° so that your feet are off the ground.
TECHNIQUE: Slowly pull yourself upwards until your chin comes over the bar. Pause and then lower your body under control.
BREATHING: Breathe out as you pull up; in as you lower.
VARIATIONS: A wide grip can be used, taking the bar either behind the neck or in front to chin-level. The effects of these variations are similar to those of the lateral pull-down and the front pull-down.
Points to note: All overhead pulling movements will stretch the spine, and so are beneficial if used after compression exercises such as squats and shoulder presses.

If you find this exercise particularly difficult, perform the eccentric (lowering) portion only, until you are strong enough to use the complete movement. Stand on a bench so you can grip the chinning bar with your bent arms. Bend your knees, take your feet off the bench and hold yourself in the upper chin-up position. Slowly lower yourself until your arms are straight, place your feet back on the bench, and stand up to repeat the movement.

Chin-up

Arm curl

MAJOR MUSCLE GROUPS WORKED: Biceps

ADDITIONAL MUSCLES USED: Brachialis, forearm flexors

STARTING POSITION: Grip a barbell, or the low pulley-bar of a Universal machine, in both hands. Use an 'undergrasp' grip. The bar should be held with the hands slightly wider than shoulder-width apart.

TECHNIQUE: Bend your arms so that the bar curls in a semicircle to a point just below your chin. Keep your wrists locked throughout the movement. Try to avoid upper-body sway, and allow the knees to bend slightly to take some of the potential strain from the spine.

Pause in the contracted position, and then slowly lower the bar until it rests on the thighs.

BREATHING: Breathe out as the bar is lifted and in as the bar is lowered.

VARIATIONS: The width of grip can be altered for personal comfort, and to alter slightly the emphasis placed on the arm muscles.

To avoid too much upper-body movement the exercise can be performed with your back against a wall and your feet slightly forward to aid stability. Alternatively, the upper arm can be supported on a padded bench-extension angled at 45° (*preacher curl*). The exercise can also be performed with two dumb-bells together (*dumb-bell curl*) or one at a time (*alternate dumb-bell curl*).

Arm curl. Ensure that you stand quite straight: this subject is leaning slightly to one side

Points to note: During the basic exercise, body sway should be avoided as this will take the work from the arm muscles. As you exercise to fatigue you will reach a sticking point in the movement: forced repetitions or 'cheating' reps (see pp. 77–78) can then be performed during the concentric phase of the movement.

Dips

MAJOR MUSCLE GROUPS WORKED: Triceps, pectorals
ADDITIONAL MUSCLES USED: Anterior deltoids, scapular muscles
STARTING POSITION: Grip a set of dipping bars with the palms of your hands facing each other. Bend your knees to 90° so that your feet come off the ground.
TECHNIQUE: Without swaying your torso, slowly bend your arms and allow your body to lower until your elbows are bent at an angle of slightly more than 90°. Hold the position for a moment – do not bounce – and then push yourself up again.
BREATHING: Breathe in as you lower yourself, and out as you push yourself up.
VARIATIONS: A wider grip will place a greater emphasis on the pectoral muscles.

Lowering yourself just before your arms lock will keep tension in your muscles and increase the intensity of the exercise.

Taking yourself down as low as possible will stretch the pectoral muscles more fully.

Dips

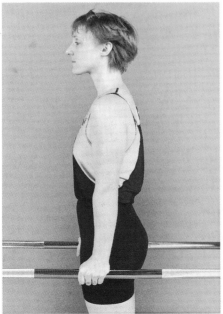

Points to note: This exercise stretches the rib-cage and places stress upon the joints between the breastbone and the ribs — the sterno-costal joints. If you fail to control the movement, dropping into the lower position, these joints can be damaged causing intense chest pain.

See page 77 for points to note on negative repetitions.

Pulley (triceps) push-downs

MAJOR MUSCLE GROUPS WORKED: Triceps

ADDITIONAL MUSCLES USED: Forearms

STARTING POSITION: Take a narrow overgrasp grip (of between 100 and 200 cm) on the 'lat' bar of the high pulley machine. Tuck your elbows into your sides, and bend them to an angle of 90°. Lean forwards slightly so that the pulley wire is close to your face.

TECHNIQUE: Moving just the forearms, press the bar down, straightening your arms and keeping your elbows tucked into your sides throughout the movement. Hold the straight position while tensing the triceps, and then slowly lower the weight until your arms are bent to 90° again.

BREATHING: Breathe out as you straighten your arms and in as they bend.

Pulley (triceps) push-down

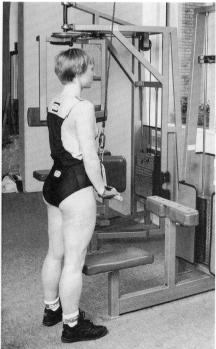

VARIATIONS: You will find a more comfortable hand position if you use a short bar that is angled down at the sides. Alternatively, you can loop a towel over the normal bar and grip this.

A power push-down can be performed, using a much heavier weight, by allowing the elbows to point out to the sides. Reverse pulley push-downs are simply performed using an undergrasp grip.

All of the exercises can be performed single-handed using the loop handle on a pulley machine.

Points to note: Shorter individuals may find it easier to raise the first weight on the machine before placing the selector pin in. This will allow the bar to rest at a lower level. Make sure that you put the weight stack back to its normal configuration before the next user comes along: if they take the pin out of the machine without holding the bar, the weights will crash down!

Triceps kick-back

MAJOR MUSCLE GROUPS WORKED: Triceps
ADDITIONAL MUSCLES USED: Posterior deltoids
STARTING POSITION: *For the right arm:-* start half-kneeling on a flat bench, with the left leg straight and the right leg bent at the knee. Support yourself with a straight left arm braced on the bench. Hold a light dumb-bell in your right hand. Bend this arm to 90°, tucking your elbow into your side. Keep your upper arm parallel with the floor.

Triceps kick-back. The subject's elbow should be tucked into the side of his body

TECHNIQUE: *For the right arm:-* Straighten your right arm, leading the movement with the end of the dumb-bell. Pause in the straight position and maximally contract the triceps. Slowly lower the dumb-bell, keeping your elbow pressed to the side of your trunk.

BREATHING: Breathe out as you straighten your arm and in as you bend it.

VARIATIONS: Altering the hand position will change the emphasis of the exercise. The movement can also be performed whilst lying on an inclined bench (*prone inclined dumb-bell kick-back*), or with a low pulley machine fitted with a loop handle (*one-arm cable kick-back*).

Points to note: This is a particularly good exercise for pre-exhausting the triceps before performing a narrow-grip bench press.

Wrist curl

MAJOR MUSCLE GROUPS WORKED: Forearm flexors

ADDITIONAL MUSCLES USED: None

STARTING POSITION: Start with your forearms resting on your knees, or over the edge of a bench leaving your hands free. Hold a light barbell with an undergrasp grip.

TECHNIQUE: Curl the bar upwards using wrist movement only. Pause, and then allow the bar to lower until the wrist is fully extended. Allow your grip to release slightly in this lower position so that the hand is stretched completely.

Wrist curl

BREATHING: Breathe normally throughout the movement.

VARIATIONS: This exercise can also be performed with the knuckles upwards and the inner surface of the forearms supported (*reverse wrist curl*) to work the forearm extensors. Both exercises can be performed single-handed with a dumb-bell (*dumb-bell wrist curl/reverse wrist curl*).

Points to note: The forearm flexors do a lot of work during a weight training programme through general gripping. The extensors are worked less, and reverse wrist curls can be used to correct this imbalance.

CHAPTER 13

The lower limb

The lower limb consists of the pelvis, the hip, the upper and lower leg bones, and the foot. Its structure is designed for locomotion: walking, running, jumping, hopping, and all other actions which move us across the ground.

The hip is a ball-and-socket joint, similar in some ways to the shoulder but much, much stronger. The joint itself is not at the side of the body but about 3 or 4 inches in. This is because the thigh bone or femur has a short 'neck', and the piece of bone you feel at the 'hip' is actually at the end of the neck of the femur and not the joint itself.

The male and female pelvis are different. The female pelvis is wider, and its muscles are generally more flexible: both features are designed to facilitate childbirth.

The large buttock muscles or *gluteals* pull the leg backwards, and also pull us back up straight after we have been leaning over to touch our toes. The hip flexor muscles pull the leg forwards in a kicking action, while the adductors pull the legs together and the abductors pull them out sideways in a scissor action. These muscles also work to stabilise the supporting limb when we stand on one leg.

The quadriceps straighten the knee; the hamstrings bend it. Both are important to the health of the knee joint. The hamstrings also pull the hip backwards, an action often neglected in weight training programmes.

The knee joint itself is very complex. It is strengthened by numerous ligaments and has special pieces of cartilage or *menisci* within it. As you move the joint, the bones actually twist in a screwing action to lock the knee straight – an action which is often the first to be lost when the knee is injured.

The calf muscles and anterior tibials (the muscles on the front of the shin) flex the foot and pull it up. The calf is used to 'push off' when running, and the anterior tibials support the foot when it is flat on the ground.

Muscles within the shin and foot itself allow the foot to perform a complex set of actions as we walk and run. As we take a step when running, the heel strikes the ground first. As the body moves forwards the outer edge of the foot takes the weight, and the foot then flattens. Finally, we push off with the ball of the big toe to propel the body forwards and start the running cycle again.

Because these events are so complex, the slightest defect can give rise to pain in the leg, hip and even the back. This is why it is so important to have a good pair of training shoes to support and cushion the foot.

The squat

MAJOR MUSCLE GROUPS WORKED: Quadriceps, buttocks, lower back
ADDITIONAL MUSCLES USED: Hamstrings, abdominals, upper body
STARTING POSITION: Stand with your feet shoulder-width apart and turned outwards slightly. The heels may be raised on a 2 cm block for comfort. The spine should be vertical, with the hips directly below the shoulders. Place a barbell across your shoulders, or the pads of a squat machine on your shoulders. You may find you need to cushion the bar with a rolled towel for comfort.
TECHNIQUE: Keep the abdominal muscles tensed to avoid excessive hollowing of the lower back. Smoothly lower yourself down, allowing your knees to travel forwards and out over your toes. Keep your spine as near vertical as possible, and do not let your backside stick out!

Stop your descent when your thighs are parallel with the ground, but do not bounce in the lower position. Straighten your legs to return to the start.
BREATHING: Breathe out as you descend; avoid holding your breath. Breathing too deeply could cause you to hyperventilate and feel lightheaded. If this occurs, replace the weight immediately and sit or lie down until you have recovered.
VARIATIONS: There are many variations on the basic squat. First,

the depth to which you descend can be altered. For example, you may perform a full, half or three-quarter squat. Second, the position of the weight can be varied. The barbell can be held in front of you, with the upper arms horizontal and arms crossed (the *front squat*), or behind you at arms' length (the *back squat*). Alternatively, dumb-bells can be held in each hand (the *dumb-bell squat*).

Points to note: This exercise compresses the spine, so movements during which the spine is stretched and decompressed should be included after the squat in a work-out (lateral pull-downs, chins and dips). Alternatively, grasp the high bar and simply hang for 30 seconds to stretch the spine. A weight training belt will help you to maintain the correct spinal position and support the abdomen during this exercise.

To help avoid knee pain try not to roll over onto the inner edge of the foot, and make sure you avoid a 'knock-kneed' posture (the knees should pass directly over the toes).

Squat

The squat machine

Step-ups

MAJOR MUSCLE GROUPS WORKED: Quadriceps
ADDITIONAL MUSCLES USED: Gluteals
STARTING POSITION: Start facing a bench which is just below knee height. Hold a light dumb-bell in each hand.
TECHNIQUE: Step up with your right leg, placing your whole foot flat on the bench. Bring your left foot up to a point alongside your right, and then step down again (leading with your right foot). Repeat the exercise for 10 reps, and then lead with the left leg for 10 reps.
BREATHING: Breathe out as you step onto the bench, and in as you step off.
VARIATIONS: This is an excellent aerobic fitness exercise when large numbers of repetitions are performed without weights (30–50).
Points to note: For safety, make sure that the whole of the foot, and not just your toes, is placed on the bench. **Lower** yourself down from the bench with each rep; do not drop down hard onto the foot. As you step up and down, try to keep the foot square and your knee directly over the foot. Try to stop yourself from rolling over onto the inside of the foot or twisting the knee.

Step-ups. The bench should normally be placed against a wall or a pillar to prevent it from slipping

 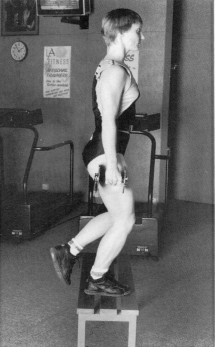

Leg press

MAJOR MUSCLE GROUPS WORKED: Quadriceps and buttocks
ADDITIONAL MUSCLES USED: Hamstrings
STARTING POSITION: *Horizontal leg press:-* start with the feet slightly turned out and positioned shoulder-width apart. Adjust the padded slide for your height and leg length. Grip the machine handles or shoulder pads. *Vertical leg press:-* start with your hips directly below your feet and your buttocks up against the vertical pad of the machine. Grip the release levers on the side of the machine, straighten your legs and twist the levers to release the weight slide.
TECHNIQUE: Slowly bend your legs as far as possible until your knees touch the sides of your chest. Without bouncing in this bottom position, slowly press your legs out straight again and repeat.
BREATHING: Breathe in as your knees bend, out as they straighten.
VARIATION: Altering the foot angle will slightly change the muscular emphasis of the exercise. When the legs are straight you can combine the exercise with a calf raise by simply pointing your toes and then returning them to the flat foot position before your knees begin to bend again.
Points to note: When your hips bend to beyond 90° your pelvis tilts and you lose the normal curve in the small of your back. Bringing the knees right up onto the chest will round the spine slightly. To avoid placing stress upon the spine, individuals

Leg press (horizontal). The knees should pass directly over the toes

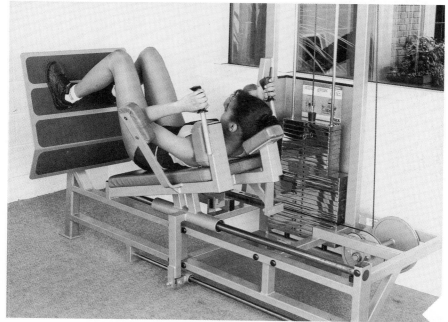

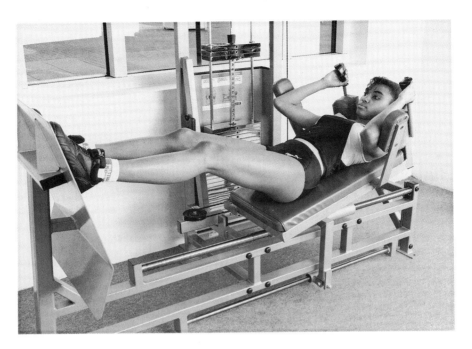

experiencing back-pain should only bend the hips and knees to 90°.

If you are using a light weight and performing large numbers of reps for endurance, be careful not to snap the knees out quickly and thus hyperextend the joint.

Lunges

MAJOR MUSCLE GROUPS WORKED: Buttocks and quadriceps of the front leg

ADDITIONAL MUSCLES USED: Quadriceps and hip flexors of back leg (stretched)

STARTING POSITION: Place a barbell across your shoulders, and stand with your feet shoulder-width apart.

TECHNIQUE: Step forward (about 0.5–0.75 m) with your right leg, bending it. Lower your body, keeping your spine as vertical as possible, until your front knee comes over the top of your foot and your back knee is about 10–15 cm above the floor. Then push yourself back forcefully to the standing position, change legs, and repeat.

BREATHING: Breathe out as you lunge forward; breathe in as you push back.

VARIATIONS: The same exercise may be performed using dumb-bells in each hand, in which case your arms should hang straight down by your sides.

The exercise may be performed without a weight but with a greater range of movement (stepping forwards to a 'full-stride' position and keeping the back leg straight). In this case the movement is predominantly a stretching exercise for the buttocks, hip flexors and upper quadriceps.

Placing the back leg on a low bench (secured against a wall so it will not slip) will increase the work done by the front leg.

Points to note: Avoid hitting your knee on the floor. If you find it difficult to control the movement, start without a weight and allow your back knee to touch onto a padded mat. Make sure that your foot is placed squarely on the floor; on lowering your body, avoid the temptation to twist the knee.

Lunge

Leg extension

MAJOR MUSCLE GROUPS WORKED: Quadriceps

ADDITIONAL MUSCLES USED: Anterior tibials

STARTING POSITION: Sit on a leg extension machine (adjusted so that the backs of your knees are against the padded end and the side of your knees are in line with the pivot point of the machine arm). Grasp the under-surface of the machine bench, or the hand grips. Hook your feet under the lower roller pads of the unit.

TECHNIQUE: Straighten your legs, and at the same time pull your toes in towards your body. Hold the locked position for 2 seconds and then slowly lower.

BREATHING: Breathe out as you straighten your legs and in as you bend them.

VARIATIONS: Pointing the toes or angling the feet inwards or outwards will change the muscular emphasis of the exercise. The intensity will be increased (but endurance reduced) if you do not lock the legs but maintain a continuous muscular tension.

Points to note: This exercise is used extensively in rehabilitation after knee injury. It has the advantage that it does not require the knee joint to take the weight of the body, and it is a controlled isolation movement.

Leg extension

The inner part of the quadriceps (*vastus medialis*) works mostly at the end-point of the movement as the knee is locked. It is essential therefore to lock the knee and to hold the point of peak contraction for a short period if the muscle is to be worked fully.

Leg curl

MAJOR MUSCLE GROUPS WORKED: Hamstrings

ADDITIONAL MUSCLES USED: Gastrocnemius of calf

STARTING POSITION: Lie face down on the leg curl machine with your knees just over the edge of the padded surface. Grip your heels under the upper pads of the machine (if it is a combined leg extension/curl unit) and hold the frame of the machine if no specific hand grips are supplied.

TECHNIQUE: Bend the knees smoothly, keeping your hips in contact with the machine surface throughout the movement. Pause in the mid position with your knees at maximum flexion. Slowly lower the weight by allowing your knees to straighten under control.

BREATHING: Breathe out as you bend your knees and in as you allow them to straighten.

VARIATIONS: The exercise can be performed using only one leg either on the same machine or standing on a separate unit (*standing leg curl*).

Changing the angle of your toes will alter the muscular emphasis of the exercise.

Leg curl

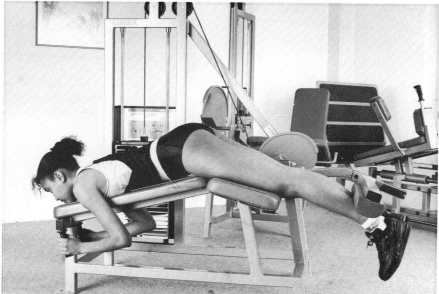

Points to note: Do not allow your pelvis to swivel while lifting; your lower back will hollow excessively and unnatural stress will be placed upon it.

If you are involved in a sport which requires a lot of sprinting, you should note two further points. First, the hamstrings both extend the hip and flex the knee, and both of these actions must be worked equally. To this effect, make sure you put some cable kickbacks in your programme. Second, the hamstrings can become very tight from leg curls, so always add some stretching exercises to your routine to compensate for this.

Cable hip abduction

MAJOR MUSCLE GROUPS WORKED: Hip abductors
ADDITIONAL MUSCLES USED: Trunk (side) flexors
STARTING POSITION: Start standing sideways at a low pulley machine. Hold onto an upright of the machine frame (not the weight guide). Place the ankle cuff around the leg furthest from the machine and keep the pulley wire taught.
TECHNIQUE: Pull your leg out sideways to an angle of about 45°; pause, and then slowly return to the starting position. As the weight lowers, your outer leg should move in front of (or behind) your inner one, to increase the range of movement.
BREATHING: Breathe out as the leg is lifted, and in as it is lowered.

VARIATIONS: By attaching the ankle cuff to your inner leg, starting from a stride position, and pulling the legs together, the hip adductors of the inner leg are worked.

Points to note: Placing the ankle cuff further up the leg (behind the calf or knee) will reduce the leverage effect of the weight and make the exercise easier. Try to confine the movement to your hips and avoid bending the spine. Also, keep the movement controlled to prevent a whipping action from building up in the leg.

Some manufacturers make a machine specifically for these exercises, in which case the ankle strap is replaced by a pad.

Hip abduction machine

Cable kick-back

MAJOR MUSCLE GROUPS WORKED: Gluteals
ADDITIONAL MUSCLES USED: Hamstrings
STARTING POSITION: Stand facing a low pulley machine, holding an upright of the machine frame (not the weight guide). Place an ankle strap around one leg, and take the slack out of the pulley wire before you start the movement.

TECHNIQUE: Keeping your torso still and upright, kick your straight leg backwards to about 30–45°. Hold the contracted position, tightening the gluteals, and then slowly return to the starting position.

BREATHING: Breathe out as you kick your leg backwards, in as your leg returns.

VARIATIONS: Facing out from the machine and kicking the straight leg forwards will work the hip flexors.

Points to note: This exercise is particularly good for toning the buttock muscles. Better results can be achieved by combining it with prone leg extensions (*see* opposite). If this exercise is carried out too quickly, using a 'whipping' action, strain is placed on the lower back. Where a specific machine is available for this exercise, the action is similar except the ankle strap is replaced by a thigh pad.

Hip extension machine

Prone leg extension

MAJOR MUSCLE GROUPS WORKED: Gluteals, lower back
ADDITIONAL MUSCLES USED: Hamstrings
STARTING POSITION: Lie face down on the floor or on a gym mat. Keep your arms by your sides, palms down.
TECHNIQUE: Slowly lift both of your legs at the same time, keeping your knees and feet pressed together. Pause in the upper position, tightening the gluteal muscles, and then slowly lower.
BREATHING: Breathe out as you lift and breathe in as you lower. Do not hold your breath.
VARIATIONS: You can perform this exercise lying over a bench, with your chest and waist supported but both legs free. From this position, with your legs lower than your torso, try to lift your legs above the horizontal. Both exercises can be made harder by gripping a small dumb-bell between your feet, and easier by bending your knees or lifting a single leg only.

Points to note: This exercise places considerable stress on the muscles of the lower spine, and some users may find it painful. Always start with the basic movement and practise strict form. If you find your back is arching excessively, tighten your abdominals to hold your pelvis in a neutral position.

These movements are very effective in toning the buttocks. They are still more effective when combined with cable kick-backs (pp. 119–120).

Lying (prone) leg extension

Calf (heel) raises

MAJOR MUSCLE GROUPS WORKED: Gastrocnemius
ADDITIONAL MUSCLES USED: Soleus
STARTING POSITION: Start standing upright, with a barbell or the pads of a squat machine across your shoulders. Stand on a block 10–15 cm high, with the ball of the foot supported and the heel over the edge of the block.
TECHNIQUE: Lower your heels, stretching your calves fully, and then slowly push up onto your toes as far as possible. Pause and then repeat.
BREATHING: Breathe out as you push up, and in as you lower.
VARIATIONS: This exercise can be performed using one leg only, with the inactive leg bent to an angle of 90° and crossed behind the active one. In this case a dumb-bell is held in one hand, the other hand touching a wall for balance.

A seated calf raise can be performed: start sitting on a chair with your feet in the same position as above. Place a weight across your knees. In this case greater emphasis is placed on the soleus, and less on the gastrocnemius.

Points to note: Calf exercises may also be performed on a leg press machine.

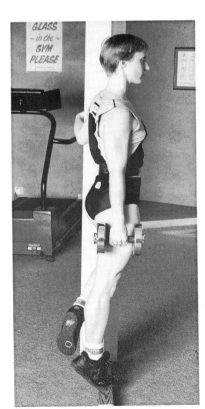

Calf (heel) raise. The subject is holding a pillar for balance

CHAPTER 14

The trunk

The main structure within the trunk is the spine. This is a flexible column of block-like bones or *vertebrae*, which protect the spinal cord and allow movement. Between successive vertebrae is a spongy disc. These discs have a gel-like centre and change shape as the spine moves.

During prolonged standing, and certain weight training exercises which compress the spine, water is squeezed out of the discs and the whole spine gets shorter. In fact, you can be about 1 cm shorter at the end of a heavy training session because of this.

At the back of each bone are two small facet joints. The various bones and joints are protected by ligaments and muscles, some of which run the whole length of the spine.

At the top of the spine is the rib-cage. Pairs of curved ribs join onto the spine at the back, and the breastbone at the front, to encircle the lungs and heart in a protective bony cage. The base of the spine forms the *sacrum*, which joins onto the pelvis via the *sacro-iliac*, a joint which plays an important part in pregnancy.

Various muscles attach from the ribs down to the pelvis. Centrally, the *rectus abdominis* attaches into the pubic bone, while on either side are located the *oblique abdominals*. The rectus flexes the spine, while the obliques twist the trunk. At the side of the trunk are the *transverse abdominals*, which act as a muscular girdle to support the contents of the abdomen. Lying either side of the spinal column are two thick muscles, the *spinal erectors*, which straighten and extend the spine.

As well as moving the spine, the various muscles in the trunk also tilt the pelvis. The abdominal muscles and the hamstrings tilt the pelvis backwards and flatten the lower spine, while the hip flexors and spinal extensors tilt the pelvis forwards and increase the hollow of the spine. Weak abdominal muscles often allow the pelvis to drop and tilt too far, so strengthening them will not only flatten the stomach but also correct your pelvic posture.

The spine itself is not straight, but has a number of natural hollows to give it 'spring'. The hollow at the base of the spine is called the *lumbar lordosis*. Maintenance of this curve is important for the prevention of pain in the lower back.

Sit-ups

MAJOR MUSCLE GROUPS WORKED: Rectus abdominis, oblique abdominals
ADDITIONAL MUSCLES USED: Hip flexors
STARTING POSITION: Lie flat on an abdominal board with your knees bent and your feet hooked under the foot-pads. Novices should place their hands by their sides; more advanced users should place them at the side of their head.
TECHNIQUE: Lift your head and shoulders first, to tense your abdominal muscles, and then sit up. Keep this curled-up position for as long as possible as you lower your back down to the starting position. The small of your back should touch the bench first, followed by your spine, and finally your shoulders.
BREATHING: Breathe out as you sit up, and in as you 'lie' back.
VARIATIONS: Hold a weight across your chest, and sit back without touching your head and shoulders to the bench. This maintains tension in the abdominal muscles, and is called a *trunk curl*.

Bend your knees to 90° and rest your calves on a flat bench. This 'trunk crunch' reduces the work done by the hip flexors and increases the emphasis on the rectus abdominis. For another variation, twist as you come up, slowly taking your right elbow towards your left knee and vice versa (*oblique crunch*). This increases the work done by the oblique abdominals.

Points to note: In the case of a straight-legged sit-up, the hip muscles pull powerfully on the lower spine and can cause pain. Performing the sit-up with the knees bent will reduce the likelihood of this occurring.

Even with the knees bent, sitting up with the lower spine off the surface of the bench, the hip flexors are being worked. These muscles are generally very strong and short as they are worked during everyday activities such as climbing stairs. To emphasise the abdominals and reduce the work done by the hip flexors, try performing all sit-up movements without the feet fixed. You will achieve shorter range but much more intense movements.

Hanging leg raises

MAJOR MUSCLE GROUPS WORKED: Hip flexors, abdominals
ADDITIONAL MUSCLES USED: Arms and shoulders
STARTING POSITION: Hang at arms' length (overgrasp) from a bar.
TECHNIQUE: Bring both of your legs up together slowly, until they are horizontal. Pause, and then lower under control. You can touch your toes briefly to the floor at the end of each rep to prevent body-sway from building up.
BREATHING: Breathe out as you lift your legs, and in as they lower.
VARIATIONS: This exercise can also be performed on a multi-gym hip-flexor unit, where your body-weight is supported on your forearms with your elbows bent to 90°.
Points to note: The exercise is easier if you bend your knees, as the leverage of the legs is thus reduced. Allowing the legs to swing backwards will hyperextend the spine and can be dangerous. This works the lower abdominals intensely (especially below the umbilicus). The exercise can be performed lying down, but the knees must stay bent and the hips flexed to 90°. The action is simply to lift the tail bone by bending the spine and tilting the pelvis.

Side-bends

MAJOR MUSCLE GROUPS WORKED: Oblique abdominals
ADDITIONAL MUSCLES USED: Other abdominal muscles
STARTING POSITION: Hold a dumb-bell in your right hand. Your left hand should be placed behind your head. Ensure that your position is stable, with your feet shoulder-width apart.
TECHNIQUE: Bend sideways to the right, allowing the dumb-bell to lower towards the floor. From this stretched position bend to the left, reaching as far over as possible in an attempt to point your free left elbow towards your left foot.

After you have done all your reps on one side, change the dumb-bell over to the other hand and repeat the exercise.
BREATHING: Breathe out as you pull the dumb-bell up.

VARIATIONS: The exercise can be performed holding the loop handle of a low pulley machine.

Points to note: Try to confine the movement to sideways bending only; do not let your torso bend forwards, and keep both knees locked.

Side-bend

Spinal hyperextensions

MAJOR MUSCLE GROUPS WORKED: Spinal extensors, hip extensors
ADDITIONAL MUSCLES USED: Shoulder retractors
STARTING POSITION: Lie flat on the floor, with your arms by your sides (novices) or at the side of your head (advanced users).
TECHNIQUE: Slowly arch your back, lifting your head, shoulders and chest from the mat. Pause and then lower under control.
BREATHING: Keep breathing steadily throughout the exercise.
VARIATIONS: At the same time as lifting the spine, lift both legs from the hips, keeping them straight.

A similar exercise can be performed on a 'roman' chair. The hips and legs are supported, and you begin the movement with your torso angled downwards.

Points to note: To work the buttock muscles very hard, perform cable pulley kick-backs immediately after this exercise. When performing the movement on a 'roman' chair, be cautious not to over-arch the spine by allowing the pelvis to tilt forwards. If this starts to happen, tighten the abdominals to bring the spine back into a more natural position, and ensure that you perform the exercise to the horizontal only.

Spinal hyperextension. This subject demonstrates a high degree of flexibility. Normally the chest and shoulders will only just lift clear of the floor

Trunk rotation

MAJOR MUSCLES WORKED: Oblique abdominals
ADDITIONAL MUSCLES USED: Hip and shoulder muscles
starting position: Sit astride a bench with an 'unloaded' weight training bar across your shoulders. An assistant should stand behind you. Make sure you are sitting upright – do not slouch.
TECHNIQUE: The assistant takes hold of the ends of the bar to provide a controlled resistance. Twist your trunk round to the right, hold the position of maximum rotation briefly, and then return to the starting position. Pause, and then twist around to the lift. Throughout the movement your assistant should resist your action but allow you to turn smoothly.
BREATHING: Breathe out as you twist and breathe in when you reach the mid-position.

VARIATIONS: Sometimes a specific machine is available for this exercise. In this case, lock your legs around the chair to provide a stable base, and place your arms onto the pads at shoulder level. As you twist, lift the weight. The obliques can also be worked lying down: bend the knees and hips to 90° and hold the arms out at shoulder level in a 'T' shape. Slowly lower the knees, first to one side and then to the other (as far as is comfortable, or until they touch the floor). Return to the mid-position and repeat the movement to the other side.

Points to note: When performing trunk rotation lying down, keep the action controlled and do not allow the knees to 'fall' to the ground. Make sure with all of the exercises that you do not hold your breath throughout the movement!

Rotary torso machine

CHAPTER 15

Practical application

This section will put together the various exercises described on pages 90–128 into example programmes. It will also look at how others may be developed according to individual needs.

Remember that there are no 'right' or 'wrong' programmes, only ones which work or do not work for you. Do not expect a programme to suit you all the time. You will have 'off' days, and will want to change your exercise routines regularly to maintain motivation. When devising your own programme you will need to look again at Chapter 5 concerning the order of exercises and muscle symmetry. You may want to concentrate on certain aspects of fitness for a few months and then change the emphasis of your training. This is where periodisation (pp. 79–80) proves useful.

On the other hand, you may find that it takes too much time to work all of your body in each work-out session. If this is the case, the split routine systems in Chapter 10 should be considered.

Determining the weight to be lifted

The weight you lift will depend on the total number of repetitions to be performed on a particular part of the body, and on the type of training you choose.

To build muscle mass you should aim to use the maximum weight you can lift for 8–10 reps, and perform only 1–2 sets. For toning programmes, perform 3–5 sets using a lighter weight for the first 2 sets and building to a maximum for the final set.

For fitness programmes you can use light weights which can be handled comfortably throughout your training programme. In addition, consider circuit training for overall fitness.

Charting your progress

Inevitably, your rate of progress will vary. Sometimes you will feel that you are making rapid gains; at other times you may feel despondent because it seems that you are making no progress. To maintain motivation you will need to see results, and you can achieve this by charting your achievements.

Record a number of body measurements, because some will change more than others depending on which fitness components you are emphasising in your programme. For example, strength gains will be rapid initially and then tail off. Body-weight may remain fairly static as muscle density increases with improved body-tone. At the same time, body-fat should reduce.

A variety of tests and measurements can be used. This book will detail just four body measurements, each recorded monthly; a variety of simple gym tests; and a fitness test. The body measurements are as follows.

- Body-weight.
- Body-fat.
- Limb/torso girth.
- Whole-body photographs.

Body-weight

This will obviously measure all the tissues of the body, not just muscle. Although it is the most popular measure of body make-up, in reality it will not give a true picture. This is because the body is made up of a number of components, including water, muscle, bone and fat. When you train, your muscles become heavier and water and fat are lost; however, your total weight may remain unchanged. If you are noticeably overweight, however, you should see some reduction.

Weigh yourself at the same time of day each time to eliminate the effects of meals and bowel habits, and always in the same clothing. Use the same scales for accuracy. Compare your weight to the charts in table 7, taking into account height and frame size.

Table 7   Body-weight relative to height and frame size (in stones/lbs.)

MEN

Height in feet/inches	Small frame	Medium frame	Large frame
5.1	8.0 – 8.8	8.6 – 9.3	9.0 –10.1
5.2	8.3 – 8.12	8.8 – 9.7	9.3 –10.4
5.3	8.6 – 9.0	8.12– 9.10	9.6 –10.8
5.4	8.9 – 9.3	9.1 – 9.13	9.9 –10.12
5.5	8.12– 9.7	9.4 –10.3	9.12–11.2
5.6	9.2 – 9.11	9.8 –10.7	10.2 –11.7
5.7	9.6 –10.1	9.12–10.12	10.7 –11.12
5.8	9.10–10.5	10.2 –11.2	10.11–12.2
5.9	10.0 –10.10	10.6 –11.6	11.1 –12.6
5.10	10.4 –11.0	10.10–11.11	11.5 –12.11
5.11	10.8 –11.4	11.0 –12.2	11.10–13.2
6.0	10.12–11.8	11.4 –12.7	12.0 –13.7
6.1	11.2 –11.13	11.8 –12.12	12.5 –13.12
6.2	11.6 –12.3	11.13–13.1	12.10–14.3
6.3	11.10–12.7	12.4 –13.8	13.0 –14.8

WOMEN

Height in feet/inches	Small frame	Medium frame	Large frame
4.8	6.8 – 7.0	6.12– 7.9	7.6 – 8.7
4.9	6.10– 7.3	7.0 – 7.12	7.8 – 8.10
4.10	6.12– 7.6	7.3 – 8.1	7.11– 8.13
4.11	7.1 – 7.9	7.6 – 8.4	8.0 – 9.2
5.0	7.4 – 7.12	7.9 – 8.7	8.3 – 9.5
5.1	7.7 – 8.1	7.12– 8.10	8.6 – 9.8
5.2	7.10– 8.4	8.1 – 9.0	8.9 – 9.12
5.3	7.13– 8.7	8.4 – 9.4	8.13–10.2
5.4	8.2 – 8.11	8.8 – 9.9	9.3 –10.6
5.5	8.6 – 9.1	8.12– 9.13	9.7 –10.10
5.6	8.10– 9.5	9.6 –10.7	10.1 –11.4
5.7	9.0 – 9.9	9.6 –10.7	10.1 –11.4
5.8	9.4 –10.0	9.10–10.11	10.5 –11.9
5.9	9.8 –10.4	10.0 –11.1	10.9 –12.0
5.10	9.12–10.8	10.4 –11.5	10.13–12.5

Body-fat

This is a more accurate method of assessing obesity. To measure body-fat you need to determine skinfold thickness. A skinfold is simply a piece of skin and fat which is pinched up and measured. Measurements are taken with special skinfold callipers which pinch the skin with a specific pressure. Figure 27 comprises the

plan for a simple skinfold calliper. Photocopy this, and stick the
copy onto a piece of thick card. Cut out the shape and fasten it
together with a clip.

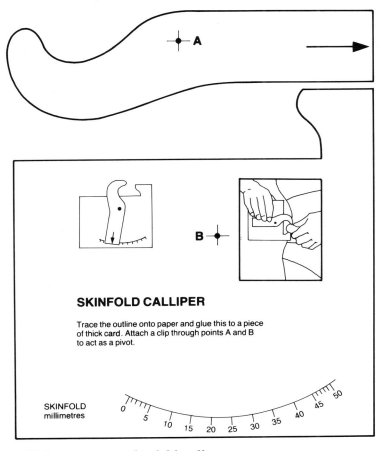

Fig. 27 *Make your own skinfold callipers*

This can be used to measure skinfold thickness at specific parts
of the body. The waist, back of the arm and thigh are useful areas.
Make sure that when you pinch the skin up you do not also pick
up muscle – tense and release the muscle underneath to be sure.

The site you use for the skinfold must be the same each time for
you to make an accurate comparison. You can be sure of this by
measuring the distance between the skinfold and a piece of bone
which juts out. For example, the waist skinfold can be 10 cm
above the point of bone on the front of the pelvis.

The amount you squeeze the skin will also have a bearing on your skinfold score, so be sure to compress the skin to the same degree with each measurement.

Limb/torso girths

In this case you can decide to measure whichever points are relevant to you. Many women choose the waist, hips, and thighs. Men wishing to lose weight generally measure the waist; for those wishing to build muscle the arm, chest and thigh may be used. Again, it is not so much *what* you measure as *how*. Make sure you choose the same site each time, and the same tape measure. Pull the tape tight but do not compress the skin (*see* fig. 28).

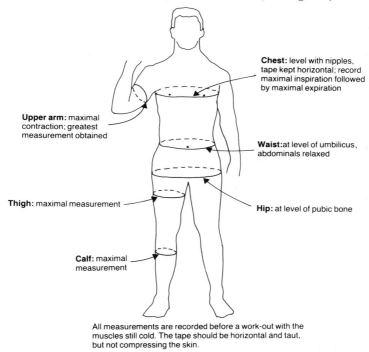

Chest: level with nipples, tape kept horizontal; record maximal inspiration followed by maximal expiration

Upper arm: maximal contraction; greatest measurement obtained

Waist: at level of umbilicus, abdominals relaxed

Thigh: maximal measurement

Hip: at level of pubic bone

Calf: maximal measurement

All measurements are recorded before a work-out with the muscles still cold. The tape should be horizontal and taut, but not compressing the skin.

Fig. 28 Girth measurements

Whole-body photographs

How you look is often the most significant motivating factor in weight training. You can photograph yourself each month, making sure that you stay at the same distance from the camera each time. Choose a front and a side-on view, and stand in front of a grid to make comparisons easier. The grid can be made simply by drawing thick lines at 6 in intervals with a felt-tip pen on the back of a length of wallpaper. Strengthen the top of the sheet with a slat of wood, and hang it on the wall behind you when you take the photo.

Gym tests

● *Strength*. Strength can be measured using the gym apparatus itself. Warm up generally first, and then specifically by performing 20 light repetitions on whichever machine you have chosen to perform the test.

Take as an example the bench press. The essential point is that you should be able to perform one repetition maximally. Obviously, the more attempts you make, the more tired you will get; so you will not be measuring your maximum strength with each attempt.

Select a weight which you think is maximal for you, and attempt to lift it. If you fail, reduce the weight. If you succeed, increase it. Rest for at least a minute, keeping yourself covered up to maintain body-heat, and then try again. The maximum weight is defined as the last lift you were able to perform before failure.

If you fail to achieve this in three or four repetitions it is best to try during another work-out, because the muscle will no longer be capable of performing maximally.

● *Muscle endurance*. To measure muscle endurance, pick a weight which you can handle comfortably. Find out the maximum number of reps you can perform with this weight in one minute. When you come to repeat the test, use the same weight. Alternatively, you could perform the maximum number of repetitions to fatigue.

● *Power*. Power can be assessed from the vertical jump (see fig. 29). Stand side-on to a wall, with your nearest arm stretched over your head. Mark with your finger the furthest point up the wall that you can reach. Then bend down and jump as high as you can, again marking the wall with your finger. Measure the distance between the two marks and then compare this with the distances shown in table 8.

It is a good idea to cover your finger with chalk dust to leave a mark that can easily be removed!

● *Flexibility*. A simple test of flexibility is the 'sit and reach' test (see fig. 30). Turn a gym bench or chair onto its side and fasten a ruler over it. Sit with your legs straight, your feet flat against the chair, and the ruler lying between your knees.

Relax and, keeping your legs straight, record how far along the ruler you can reach. Then reach forwards in one strong movement, keeping your knees and elbows locked, and try to touch your toes.

Table 8   Vertical jump rating scale in cm

		Men		
Rating	Age 15–20	20–30	30–40	40–50
Poor	32	38	36	30
Fair	42	48	45	38
Average	50	54	52	44
Good	55	60	57	50
Excellent	60	65	62	56
		Women		
Rating	Age 15–20	20–30	30–40	40–50
Poor	30	32	25	20
Fair	38	40	32	25
Average	42	44	40	32
Good	50	52	46	40
Excellent	55	57	52	46

Fig. 29 Vertical jump test   Fig. 30 The 'sit and reach' test

Do not bounce. Hold the movement for 2 seconds, recording the new point along the ruler. Your 'sit and reach' score is the difference between your starting point and the furthest point you reached. Compare your figure with table 9.

Table 9 **'Sit and reach' rating scale in cm**

Rating	Men/Boys cm	Women/Girls cm
Excellent	32+	34+
Good	24–31	26–33
Average	17–23	17–25
Poor	9–16	9–16
Very Poor	8 and below	8 and below

The fitness test

The speed at which your heart rate returns to normal after exercising (heart rate recovery) is a measure of your fitness. The step test uses this fact as follows.

Use a standard gym bench or chair 16 in high. Men should step up and down 24 times per minute and women 22 times per minute for a total of 5 minutes (or until you feel comfortably tired). It is easiest to use a count of 'up 2, 3, 4', counting each time the right leg steps up.

When you finish, sit down exactly one minute after the exercise and record your pulse for 30 seconds. Do the same 2 minutes and then 3 minutes after exercise; you should see your pulse rate slowing. Add all of these pulse rates together to get your total pulse.

Your fitness score can then be calculated by multiplying the duration of the exercise in seconds (the full 5 minutes is 300 seconds) by 100 and dividing this value by your total pulse score multiplied by two.

Example

A male exercised by stepping 24 times per minute for a total of 5 minutes. His pulse scores, recorded for 30 seconds each at 1, 2 and 3 minutes after exercise, were 85, 70, and 58 respectively. His fitness score is calculated as follows.

$$\text{Fitness score} = \frac{\text{Exercise duration (seconds)} \times 100}{2 \times \text{total pulse score}}$$

$$= \frac{300 \times 100}{2 \times (85 + 70 + 58)} = \mathbf{70.4}$$

Keep a record of your fitness scores each month to chart your progress. A guide to your rating is shown in table 10.

Table 10 Step-test fitness rating

90 and over	Excellent
80–89	Good
65–79	Average
55–64	Poor
54 and below	Very poor

Weight training programmes

The following comprise examples of various weight training programmes which suit some common requirements. In the case of all the programmes you should first perform an adequate warm-up, and then include stretching exercises as a 'cool-down' when the session is finished.

Start with light poundages until you are used to the various routines, and then increase the weight with each work-out as you progress. Remember it is important continually to overload the muscle. As you grow stronger and your muscles tone up, unless you increase the weight lifted you are actually not working as hard as when you first started your training programme.

Remember also that the way to assess the desired weight and number of repetitions is simple. If you are to perform 15 reps, and you are only able to lift a certain weight 5 times, it is too heavy. If you can lift it 20 times, it is too light. With experience you will get to know what weight is suitable. With multi-stack apparatus the advantage is that you can change the weight in mid-set.

General fitness

Cycle/jog on spot	5 mins
Bench press	15
Squat	15
Sit-up (knees bent)	15
Dumb-bell lift	15
Star jump	25
Side-bend	15 (each side)
Lateral pull-down	15
Hip scissor	15
Spinal extension	15

Body toning for women

Bench press	15
Dumb-bell lateral raise	15

Lateral pull-down	15
Lunge (no weight)	12 (each leg)
Hip scissor	15 (each leg)
Reverse leg lift	15
Sit-up (knees bent)	15 (slow emphasis)
Side bend	15 (each side)

Waist toning and fitness for men

Bench press	15
Shoulder press	15
Arm curl	12
Seated rowing	15
Sit-up (knees bent)	15 (slow emphasis)
Hip flexor	10 (slow emphasis)
Sit-up (knees bent)	15 (slow emphasis)
Hip flexor	15 (slow emphasis)
Side-bend	15 (each side)
Step-up	15 (each leg)
Leg extension	15

Bodybuilding

Chest press	15/12/10
(30–60 sec rest between sets)	
Dumb-bell flye	12/10/08
Shoulder press	12/10/08
Lateral raise	10/08/06
Squat	15/12/10
Calf raise	15/15
Lateral pull-down	12/10/08
Dips	Max.
Chins	Max.

Racket sports

Step-up	25 (each leg)
Shoulder press	15/12
Sit-up (knees bent)	Max. for 1 min
Lunge	15 (each leg)
Lateral pull-down	15/12
Dumb-bell flye	12/10
Spinal extension	15/12
Vertical jump	Max. for 1 min
Calf raise	25/25

Football/rugby

Light squat	20
Calf raise	20
Hip abductor	15 (each leg)
Sit-up & twist	15
Reverse leg raise	15
Shoulder press	15
Seated rowing	15
Leg extension	12/10
Side-bend	15 (each side)
Alternate leg thrust	2 mins

Road running

Chest press	15
Seated rowing	12
Lateral dumb-bell raise	12
Lateral pull-down	15
Arm curl	10
Triceps push-down	10
Leg extension	15/12
Sit-up (knees bent)	15
Side-bend	15 (each side)
Spinal extensions	15

Rehabilitation/re-strengthening programmes

Never use weights within four days of an injury occurring, or while the joint is still swollen. Always apply weight training with caution. The level of pain can be used as a general guide to the suitability of the exercise programme. You must distinguish between the ache of normal training and pain through excessive stress on the damaged part of the body. As a general rule, never exercise through increasing pain. If pain occurs and then improves with exercise, that is fine; it may be just stiffness working itself loose. If the pain increases, stop training and rest immediately. Try again the next day; if the pain recurs then it is likely that the exercise is too intense for the stage of healing.

Perform all exercises slowly and only after a thorough warm-up. Always check with your doctor or physiotherapist before beginning an exercise programme after injury.

Knee re-strengthening

Week one/two

Leg extension (5 sec hold)	15
Leg curl	15
Bench press	12
Lateral pull-down	12
Hip adduction	10 each leg
Hip abduction	10 each leg
Lying leg extension	15
Lateral raise	12
Trunk curl	15

Week two/three

$\frac{1}{4}$ squat holding dipping frame	10
Leg extension	(5 sec hold)
Leg curl	15
Cable kick-back	15
Heel raise	15
Shoulder press	12
Seated rowing	15
Triceps extension	12
Trunk curl with twist	15

Back re-strengthening

Week one/two

Spinal extension (limited range with isometric hold)	15
Trunk curl	10
Lateral pull-down	15
Seated rowing	12
Bench press	12
Lunge	10 (each leg)

Week three/four

Spinal extension on bench	15
Trunk curl	15
Spinal extension on bench	15
Trunk curl	15
Side-bend	10 (each side)
Lateral pull-down	15
Seated rowing	15
$\frac{1}{2}$ squat (light)	10
Heel raise (dumb-bell)	15

CHAPTER 16

Troubleshooting

A thorough warm-up and a good exercise technique will go a long way towards preventing injuries. However, we are all human; mistakes in training and accidents in the gym are a risk that we all take. When an injury occurs, the action immediately subsequent is an important factor in determining the recovery time. For this reason a knowledge of basic sports first-aid is essential, and everyone involved in teaching in a gym, at whatever level, should be encouraged to hold a first-aid certificate and a relevant coaching/ training award.

Injury and healing

When the body is injured, the response of the tissues is always similar; only the intensity of the reaction will vary. Any injury, whether it be a simple sprain or a major fracture, will result in inflammation. This process causes the body to react in such a way that specific changes are noticeable, and these are referred to as the 'cardinal signs of inflammation'. The signs are redness, swelling, heat and pain, all of which join together to lead to impaired function (see fig. 31).

Take the example of an ankle sprain. While walking in the gym you trip over a dumb-bell that someone has left on the floor. Your foot is turned violently inwards, overstretching and tearing the ligaments on the outside of the ankle. This injury breaks some of the smaller blood vessels in the area and releases blood. This in

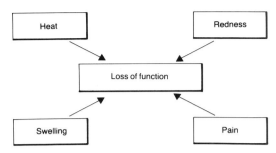

Fig. 31 *Signs of inflammation*

turn causes the skin covering the injury to appear hot and red. The
release of blood upsets the delicate balance of tissue fluids and so
swelling builds up under the skin. Pain results from the pressure of
the accumulating swelling and blood, and from irritation caused by
chemicals released at the time of injury. The ankle – now hot, red,
swollen and painful – cannot be moved properly and function is
impaired.

To try to 'train through' this type of injury is pointless, even if it
were possible; the damaged tissues would tear further and the
swelling would spread. The necessary action can be summarised by
the simple pneumonic PRICE, standing for:

P – Protect
R – Rest
I   – Ice
C – Compress
E – Elevate

The first thing we must do is protect the ankle from further
injury. This involves avoiding exercise, and in some cases using a
splint or crutches to make sure that weight is not placed on the
injured part. Having protected the area, our major concern is then
to limit the formation and spread of swelling. Swelling is a glue-
like fluid which moves into the surrounding tissues and sticks
them down, causing stiffness. Often, even when the injury itself
has healed, the swelling remains and causes further problems.

Swelling will still be forming for the first 24–48 hours after
injury (the acute phase), so we must try to limit the spread of
swelling as much as possible by resting during this time. Later on
(the sub-acute phase), no fresh swelling will form, and the problem
is how to gradually break up the sticky swelling which is already

there without disturbing the newly healing tissues. At this stage, very gentle movements are called for. Total rest is rarely required: what we should aim at is 'functional rest', which avoids stressing the injured tissues but allows other movements to occur normally. In the case of our injured ankle we should limit the inward movement of the ankle with a strapping, but allow the normal upward and downward motions required for normal walking.

Because blood vessels were damaged, the tissues in the immediate area will be starved of oxygen and nutrients and so will die. To limit the damage we apply ice or cold to the area to place the tissues into a sort of 'suspended animation'. This will also have the effect of limiting the pain. Swelling is spreading, so to limit this we must compress the area with an elastic bandage and elevate the foot (in the case of our swollen ankle). The PRICE action is continued regularly throughout the acute phase of the injury, applying ice every 2–3 hours of the waking day.

As we move into the sub-acute phase no fresh swelling is forming. The aim now is to get the ankle moving and speed up the healing process, at the same time making the healing tissues stronger. Now is the time to begin very gentle, controlled exercise. Heat is used instead of ice, to bring fresh blood into the area. In cases of persistent swelling, hot and cold in the form of 'contrast bathing' is useful as it opens and closes the local blood vessels in a pumping action. The injured foot is placed for 2–3 minutes in comfortably hot water, and then for the same period of time into iced water. The process is repeated over a 10–15-minute period.

The exercise should be both gentle and progressive. This means not jumping straight back into training, but starting with light movements which do not hurt, and gradually making the actions harder in order to build up the demand placed on the ankle. In total it may take 3–4 weeks for the ankle to heal completely.

Types of injury

Sports injuries generally fall into one of two common categories, **sprains** and **strains**. A sprain is an injury to a ligament, while a strain is a muscle injury. A ligament supports the joint but cannot contract, whereas a muscle moves the joint. To determine which is injured, two tests are used. If someone moves your joint as you keep the muscles relaxed (passive movement), and this causes pain, it is likely that the ligament is affected. If the joint stays still as you tense the muscles against a resistance (resisted movement), and this causes pain, it is more likely that the muscle is affected. Obviously a great many structures could be affected, and to get an accurate diagnosis you must see your physiotherapist or doctor.

There are three grades of injury. Grade one injuries are very mild, with only slight tissue damage. These really represent an overstretching of the tissue rather than true damage, and they heal fairly quickly if treated correctly. The grade two injury is more serious because it involves a greater amount of tissue damage and the release of blood and swelling. If the tissue breaks (ruptures) completely, a very serious grade three injury has occurred.

The type of treatment will depend largely on the severity of injury. Grade one injuries require a short period of complete rest (one or two days), followed by a gentle return to activity. The affected area is slightly stiff and will require gentle stretching exercises. It will also be weaker, so you should reduce the amount of weight you use on the exercises which affect the injured part. Grade two injuries require more specialist treatment from a physiotherapist; this may involve soft tissue manipulation, electrotherapy and special exercises to get you into a position where you can resume gentle supervised training. Grade three injuries frequently require hospital treatment (sometimes even surgery), intense rehabilitation and a cautious return to sport.

The gentle return to sport

Following an injury, exercise must be started gradually, using a technique known as 'progressive exercise therapy' (PET). To go from complete rest back into full training is simply asking for trouble and the injury will almost certainly recur. When dealing with injury to the lower limb, exercise should begin without the foot on the ground (non-weight-bearing), and progress gradually to movements where the foot is placed on the ground but the body-weight supported (partial-weight-bearing). Finally, all the body-weight can be taken (full-weight-bearing). In the case of our injured ankle, the ankle should be moved up and down and inwards and outwards while sitting on the floor with the leg outstretched. As strength improves, the foot is placed on the floor and the same actions carried out while sitting and then standing holding onto something. Eventually, full-weight-bearing exercises such as heel raises and light squats are used. The number of repetitions and the weight used is gradually increased at each training session, all the time taking note of how the injured part feels. Anything which causes pain has pushed the limb too far.

All the components of fitness should be used. Flexibility will be limited, so stretching exercises must be put into the training programme. Muscle endurance will have been lost in cases of muscle strains, so some exercises should involve low-weight, high-repetition work to build up endurance. Power and speed are generally the last fitness components to return. Because these involve fast actions they must be used with caution. However, to over-protect the injury and not use power/speed training will leave the injured area open to further problems and is a frequent cause of re-injury.

Cramp and stitch

Muscle cramps or spasms can occur if a muscle is contracted in its shortened position and held for any length of time. When this occurs the muscle will not relax, and to relieve the pain the area should be stretched. The stretch should be exactly opposite to the action which caused the cramp, and should be applied slowly and held for 30 seconds. Pulling vigorously and trying to 'break' the cramp can cause muscle damage.

If an athlete suffers from persistent cramps there is normally an underlying cause. One factor is training technique. Too many 'concentration' exercises on muscles that are already short can be a cause, as can a general lack of flexibility. Stretching exercises must be used if the training programme is to be balanced.

Another possible cause is diet. Low levels of fluids, glucose and electrolytes (tissue salts) can be a factor in persistent cramps. For this reason athletes are encouraged to take small but frequent amounts of fluid throughout a work-out. Water is normally sufficient, but in a very hot environment a little sugar and salt may be added or fruit juice used. Electrolyte drinks can be useful, but athletes should be cautious about the claims made for some drinks.

A stitch is a pain in the upper abdomen which usually occurs when training is carried out on a full stomach. The exact cause is not known, but a number of possibilities have been discussed. The weight of the food in the stomach pulls on the tissue which holds the stomach and intestines in place, and may cause very slight inflammation and bleeding. Changes in blood flow to the diaphragm and internal organs is another possibility. Some relief can be found by encouraging the abdomen to move as you breathe. As you take a deep breath the abdomen should be allowed to protrude, and as you breathe out, the abs are pulled inwards. This has the effect of encouraging diaphragmatic movement. Prevention is obviously better, and athletes should not train within one or two hours of a heavy meal.

Muscle pain

Two types of muscle pain generally occur: the 'burn' felt at the time of training; and the ache occurring some days afterwards. Muscle burn is caused by *ischaemia*, or a reduction in blood flow to the working muscle. As a muscle contracts and bulges it cuts off its own blood supply. This starves the muscle of oxygen and nutrients and allows lactic acids and other chemicals to build up in the muscle tissue. These chemicals irritate the nerves which supply the muscle, giving the burning sensation. Eventually all the nutrients are used and so much acid builds up that the muscle is unable to contract and fatigue sets in. Rest is needed to allow fresh blood to flush through the area, bringing in oxygen and nutrients with it and taking away the waste chemicals. Gentle massage and warmth can aid this process.

Muscle ache occurring a few days after training is called 'delayed onset muscle soreness' or DOMS. This occurs because with intense training (especially eccentric or 'negative' weight training) some of the muscle tissue is actually damaged. This micro-damage gives rise to local inflammation and swelling which builds up gradually over a 24–48 hour period and causes pain. Again, heat from a shower or sauna and gentle massage or very light exercise will increase the blood flow to the area and reduce the pain. Because the muscle is inflamed no heavy training should be done until the DOMS has died down.

An athlete must make sure that he can distinguish between the pain of ischaemic muscle and DOMS, and that of injury. Generally, muscle pain from training occurs slowly and builds in intensity. It also occurs on both sides of the body and is general to the areas which have been worked. Pain from injury may occur suddenly if something is felt to 'go', and is usually local to one side of the body and to a single area. If you are unsure which is which, it is always best to err on the side of caution and stop training.

Joint pain

Some athletes complain of pain in the joints after training. This should always be investigated to ensure that there is no specific injury. If the pain occurs persistently and does not respond to training modifications, blood tests may be required to eliminate the possibility of joint disease. Assuming there is no underlying medical problem, the most likely cause is hyperextension of the joints — that is, overextending them and/or extending them too rapidly.

When a limb is extended, tightness in the ligaments and muscles surrounding the joint normally locks the limb in a straight position. However, in some people the joints are particularly lax, and the joint will actually straighten too far and start to bend the other way. This is most noticeable in the knee and elbow, and is made worse if the athlete has a tendency to 'snap' the arm or leg straight. The combination of rapid movement and joint laxity can stress the joint, causing swelling and pain.

Hyperextension can also occur if the weight pulls the limb too far when lowered in an uncontrolled fashion (during a preacher curl, for example). Alternatively, it may happen in exercises such as the leg press and bench press, where momentum builds up in the weight and the limb is pulled too far at the end point of the exercise.

Pain can occur from jarring of the joints. This is common in exercises such as step-ups and lunges, where the foot is stamped to the ground as the weight is lowered by the legs. It may also occur in the bench and shoulder presses if the weight is 'thrown' up rather than lifted under control. If the action is too rapid, the weight may leave the hand for a split second and return with a jolt, forcing the wrist to extend too far and compressing the wrist structures.

The treatment of joint pain of this type should be rest, ice and compression until the pain and inflammation have subsided. Later, exercise technique must be modified to remove the causal factor.

Skin conditions

The normal skin problems facing the weight-trained athlete are calluses and blisters on the hands resulting from training, cuts and grazes from injury, and foot problems from the changing room. Both calluses and blisters occur for the same reason – friction on the skin surface. If friction occurs over a number of short periods the skin will thicken and harden to form a callus. If friction occurs in one long bout, the skin does not have time to adapt and harden and so fluid is released between the skin layers to act as a pad, and a blister forms.

Blisters can be treated by piercing them from the side with a sterile needle (this is best carried out by a nurse) and then placing a sterile dressing on top. Calluses may be removed using a pumice stone or sanding. In either case treatment is only effective if the cause is removed. In the case of skin calluses and blisters, padded weight training gloves should be used to reduce the friction on the skin.

Small cuts and abrasions should be washed in running water and covered with a sterile dressing. Deeper cuts should be treated in a hospital casualty department. It is easy to take these minor skin injuries far too lightly. The skin forms a protective barrier for the body, and when the skin surface is broken infection can follow. This is particularly the case in a gym where there may be sweat, dust, oil, and metal flakes on surfaces. This is why good hygiene is vital. Always take a towel into the gym and place it on a bench before you lie down. If you do leave a patch of sweat on a machine, wipe it off!

Other significant conditions are those which affect the feet, especially athletes' foot and verrucas. Athletes' foot is a fungal infection which is prevalent in hot, moist areas. The skin between the toes becomes soggy and flaky, and the condition may spread to the whole foot in severe cases. Various ointments are available from the chemist to treat and prevent this problem, and good foot hygiene, including thorough drying of the skin and the application of an anti-fungal talcum powder, is essential. A verruca is caused by a virus which enters the skin of the foot through a small cut or crack. A small hard area resembling a callus is formed, but on close inspection the centre of the wart is dark. Because the virus spreads quickly, anyone with a verruca should wear a plastic sock in the changing room. Again, a number of treatments are available from the chemist. With all foot problems athletes should see a chiropodist.

Back-pain

Back-pain is potentially a very serious condition, both because of the pain and disability caused in the short term, and because the condition has a high incidence of recurrence and can so easily turn into a long-term, chronic ailment. For these reasons, anyone suffering even the slightest bout of backache should go and see a physiotherapist straight away. This can often correct the underlying mechanisms which cause the condition and 'nip it in the bud'.

As we saw in Chapter 7 (pp. 56–68), various factors can place stress on the spine in the gym. Repeated bending and lifting will dramatically increase the leverage affecting the lower spine. In addition, many weight training exercises actually compress the discs in the base of the spine, squeezing water from them and making them shrink. Also culpable are fast, uncontrolled movements which can tear at the spinal tissues. Prevention must aim at addressing all of these factors, and good training technique is essential.

If pain should occur in the back, rest immediately. Never try to train through the pain, because if a disc is affected or a nerve trapped you will almost certainly increase any damage. Keep the spine as straight as possible and support it with a tight belt around the waist until you are able to get to a place where you can lie down. Apply ice to the area to reduce the pain and inflammation. On no account slump in a easy chair or have a hot bath: both of these actions feel good at the time, but when you try to get up from the chair or out of the bath you will get severe pain. If you must sit down, sit on a hard dining chair and place a small cushion or rolled towel in the base of your spine to support it. One of the best resting positions is on the floor with your knees bent. Sleep on a firm bed or some blankets on the floor to keep the spinal structures in line and allow them to heal. If you sleep on your side with your knees bent up, place a pillow under the upper knee to stop the spine from twisting.

In cases where you experience a dull ache which builds up slowly, rather than a sudden bout of pain, you should try to arch the spine backwards a number of times. Stand up and place your hands in the small of your back. From this position, bend backwards so you can look at the ceiling and then come back to standing. Do this movement five or ten times until the pain starts to ease and you feel only a local warmth in the small of the back. If you experience any pain spreading down the leg, stop immediately.

Dizzy spells and fainting

In the gym, dizziness usually occurs when your blood pressure drops suddenly. At any one time the body has too little blood to fill all of its blood vessels and still get blood to the brain in the standing position. To allow for this, certain blood vessels will close and others open. For example, after a meal the blood vessels around the digestive organs open while those supplying the muscles close. With exercise, the reverse occurs: the muscle blood vessels open and the digestive ones close – one cause of indigestion if you train immediately after eating a heavy meal!

The opening and closing of the blood vessels is controlled by muscles within the vessel walls. Sometimes the messages going from the brain to these vessels are confused and all the blood vessels open at once. The result is that insufficient blood gets to the brain and you feel dizzy or faint. This can occur if you get up suddenly from exercising in a lying position, or after exercises where you breathe too heavily (hyperventilate). Examples of these two situations are abdominal exercises and heavy squats. If you should feel dizzy, sit down or preferably lie down on your side to make it easier for blood to get to the brain. If someone does faint in the gym, lie them down near an open window for fresh air and on no account try to give them anything to eat or drink as they could choke.

Epilepsy

When epilepsy or 'a fit' occurs, there is a sudden loss of consciousness, usually accompanied by convulsions. There are various types of epilepsy. Some people simply become distant or unconscious for a few seconds and then come round. This sort of epilepsy generally goes unnoticed. The more apparent type causes a person to fall to the ground, sometimes making a strange sound. They may then go rigid, and the lips and mouth can go blue. After this the muscles relax and they start to convulse. Breathing may stop and they may start to froth at the mouth, clenching their teeth together. If they bite their tongue or lips, blood may appear at the mouth. The muscles controlling the bladder are sometimes affected and the person loses bladder control. Finally, they become unconscious and will then slowly come round, feeling dazed.

If this should happen in your gym, do not panic; the condition looks more serious than it actually is. Clear a space so the athlete does not hurt him or herself when they convulse. Move benches and weights out of the way. Place something soft beneath their head – a towel or a rolled-up piece of clothing is fine. If the person is biting their tongue, something should be placed between their teeth, such as a piece of rolled cloth. Do not try to hold the person down as this can make the fit worse, and on no account try to give them anything to eat or drink. There is normally no need to send for an ambulance if the person recovers completely and is used to having fits, although they may wish to see their doctor.

Diabetes

A diabetic athlete is unable to produce enough of the hormone insulin. A lack of this insulin causes the way in which the body balances the amount of sugar in the blood to be disturbed. Diabetic individuals can therefore suffer from too little sugar in the blood (*hypoglycaemia*), or from too much (*hyperglycaemia*).

Both of these situations can be dangerous, but the more usual situation in sport is hypoglycaemia. This can occur suddenly, because diabetics have to be careful about the amount of sugar they eat and often have to give themselves insulin injections regularly. Should they miss an injection, or eat too little food but still exercise intensely, they may start having problems. Normally they will feel lightheaded and become confused. They may start to sweat profusely and go pale, and their pulse may get very rapid. In some cases they will start to tremble. If they lose consciousness they should be taken straight to hospital. If they are conscious and simply feeling unwell, they should be given a sugary drink. However, if they fail to improve, a doctor should still be contacted.

Index